# A Literature Guide

## Written by Linda DeGeronimo and Anne Diehl

### for

# Harry Potter and the Sorcerer's Stone

a novel by J. K. Rowling

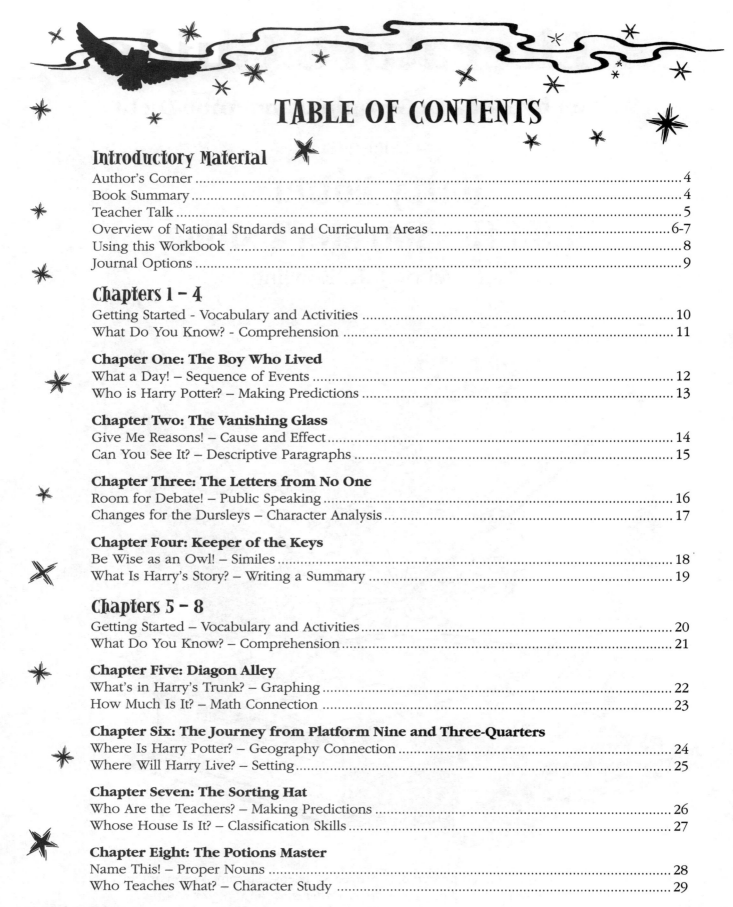

# TABLE OF CONTENTS

## Introductory Material

Author's Corner ........................................................................................................4
Book Summary ........................................................................................................4
Teacher Talk ............................................................................................................5
Overview of National Stndards and Curriculum Areas .......................................6-7
Using this Workbook .............................................................................................8
Journal Options ......................................................................................................9

## Chapters 1 – 4

Getting Started - Vocabulary and Activities .........................................................10
What Do You Know? - Comprehension ...............................................................11

**Chapter One: The Boy Who Lived**
What a Day! – Sequence of Events ......................................................................12
Who is Harry Potter? – Making Predictions .........................................................13

**Chapter Two: The Vanishing Glass**
Give Me Reasons! – Cause and Effect .................................................................14
Can You See It? – Descriptive Paragraphs ...........................................................15

**Chapter Three: The Letters from No One**
Room for Debate! – Public Speaking ...................................................................16
Changes for the Dursleys – Character Analysis ...................................................17

**Chapter Four: Keeper of the Keys**
Be Wise as an Owl! – Similes ..............................................................................18
What Is Harry's Story? – Writing a Summary .......................................................19

## Chapters 5 – 8

Getting Started – Vocabulary and Activities .........................................................20
What Do You Know? – Comprehension ...............................................................21

**Chapter Five: Diagon Alley**
What's in Harry's Trunk? – Graphing ...................................................................22
How Much Is It? – Math Connection ...................................................................23

**Chapter Six: The Journey from Platform Nine and Three-Quarters**
Where Is Harry Potter? – Geography Connection ................................................24
Where Will Harry Live? – Setting .........................................................................25

**Chapter Seven: The Sorting Hat**
Who Are the Teachers? – Making Predictions ......................................................26
Whose House Is It? – Classification Skills .............................................................27

**Chapter Eight: The Potions Master**
Name This! – Proper Nouns .................................................................................28
Who Teaches What? – Character Study ................................................................29

# TABLE OF CONTENTS

## Chapters 9 – 12

Getting Started – Vocabulary and Activities .................................................. 30
What Do You Know? – Comprehension ...................................................... 31

**Chapter Nine: The Midnight Duel**

Be an Inventor – Poetry Connection .......................................................... 32
What Does It Mean? – Figurative Language ................................................ 33

**Chapter Ten: Halloween**

How Do They Feel? – Mood ...................................................................... 34
What a Game! – Compare and Contrast ...................................................... 35

**Chapter Eleven: Quidditch**

It's a Mystery! – Draw Conclusions .......................................................... 36
Go Team Go! – Art Connection .................................................................. 37

**Chapter Twelve: The Mirror of Erised**

Play a Game! – Creative Thinking .............................................................. 38
Your Deepest Desire – Writing Connection ................................................ 39

## Chapters 13 – 17

Getting Started – Vocabulary and Activities .................................................. 40
What Do You Know? – Comprehension ...................................................... 41

**Chapter Thirteen: Nicolas Flamel**

Back in Time – History Connection ............................................................ 42
Be an Author! – Creative Writing .............................................................. 43

**Chapter Fourteen: Norbert the Norwegian Ridgeback**

Peculiar Pets – Science Connection ............................................................ 44
What an Adventure! – Creative Writing ...................................................... 45
Dragons in Romania! – Geography Connection ............................................ 46

**Chapter Fifteen: The Forbidden Forest**

What's Lurking in the Dark? – Science Connection ...................................... 47
Legendary Beasts – Mythology Connection .................................................. 48
What's Their Secret? – Making Predictions ................................................ 49

**Chapter Sixteen: Through the Trapdoor**

Magical Mush – Science Connection .......................................................... 50
The Puzzler – Math Connection ................................................................ 51

**Chapter Seventeen: The Man with Two Faces**

What Is the Truth? – Making Predictions .................................................... 52

**Final Assessment**

Open-Ended Questions and Optional Final Journal Entry Topics ...................... 53-54
Answer Key ............................................................ 55-64 & inside back cover

# Author's Corner

J. K. Rowling, a former teacher and mother of one daughter, has always been interested in writing. She wrote her first story about a rabbit at the age of six (still unpublished). She got the idea for writing the Harry Potter books while traveling by train from Manchester to London, England. Notes for the first book were written on scraps of paper as she sat at a local café. With the assistance of a grant from the Scottish Arts Council, Ms. Rowling finished *Harry Potter and the Sorcerer's Stone* and outlined plans for the next six books. Since then, Rowling's first novel has become an international hit. It received the British Book Awards for Children's Book of the Year and the Nestlé® Smarties Prize, a prestigious British children's books award which is chosen by a panel of adults and children. It also garnished the number one spot on *The New York Times* book list for several weeks.

# Book Summary

In *Harry Potter and the Sorcerer's Stone*, Harry is introduced as a young orphan who lives with his not-so-kind aunt and uncle, and his mean, spoiled cousin. His sleeping quarters are in a cupboard under the stairs, and his life is quite dismal until he starts receiving strange letters just prior to his eleventh birthday. Everything changes when Harry discovers that he is a wizard and has been invited to attend Hogwarts, a school for young witches and wizards. Once at Hogwarts, Harry's life changes and his adventures begin. He discovers that he is famous in the wizard world because he survived the night the dark wizard, Voldemort, killed his parents. At Hogwarts, Harry makes new friends; is introduced to Quidditch, a wizard flying game; and gets to study magic, charms, potions, and spells. Along with his friends, Harry also discovers a secret in the Hogwarts castle. With their help, he finds the courage to face and triumph over evil.

# Teacher Talk

Welcome to the wonderful world of Harry Potter! This comprehensive workbook has been designed for teachers using J.K. Rowling's first book, *Harry Potter and the Sorcerer's Stone*, as a teaching tool. By taking advantage of the tremendous enthusiasm for Harry Potter, and providing students with some truly exciting, fun, and creative activities which build on the skills they may already have, **A Literature Guide for *Harry Potter and the Sorcerer's Stone*** can assist you in making wonderful connections across the curriculum and maintaining student excitement for independent reading. The pages are reproducible and can be used in your classroom at your discretion (see *Journal Options,* page 9).

The format of this literature guide is user-friendly and follows a consistent pattern. Each chapter of this workbook encompasses 4-5 different chapters of *Harry Potter and the Sorcerer's Stone.* Each workbook chapter begins with vocabulary and comprehension pages. We recommend that you use these pages in a manner consistent with the level at which your students operate. For example, some advanced students and older classes may be able to answer comprehension questions in a test format when they have finished reading the chapters, while others may need to tackle them in a group and/or open-book after reading the text.

Each workbook chapter also includes 2-3 curriculum-related activities. Activities may touch on the areas of Language Arts, Math, Science, Social Studies, or Art. In addition, you will find that this workbook allows for mini-lessons by the teacher, as well as cooperative study among the students, which is thought by many experts to be one of the best ways for students to learn. By using all of these connections, as well as changing the activities to fit both independent and group learners, you will find that you are able to address many levels of learning. No type of learner is left out of this workbook.

Finally, if you have not yet read *Harry Potter and the Sorcerer's Stone*, do so quickly, and join the millions of children and adults alike who are fans of this wonderful series. We're sure you will enjoy using this workbook in your classroom, and we hope that you will be amazed at the enthusiasm of your students as they experience J. K. Rowling's world of wizardry.

Our simple suggestion: **HAVE FUN!**

# Overview of National Standards and Curriculum Areas

"All states and schools will have challenging and clear standards of achievement and accountability for all children, and effective strategies for reaching those standards." In response to this statement from the U.S. Department of Education, national education organizations such as the National Council of Teachers of English, the National Council of Teachers of Mathematics, the National Academies of Science, and National Council for the Social Studies, have created various sets of curricular standards to serve as guides for teachers and school administrators. Standards have been adopted for Language Arts, Math, Science, Social Studies, Technology, Health and Physical Education, and Fine Arts.

The standards stress the development of higher-level thinking skills through an integrated, exploratory approach. Solving problems, thinking creatively, making inferences, and drawing conclusions are considered integral components of student learning.

The activities in this workbook are designed to meet many of the achievement standards and guidelines supported by state and national education organizations. The activities have been tested in intermediate-grade classrooms, and have been embraced by teachers and students. The activities encourage students to become active learners who cooperate on complex, multisensory exercises.

Not only do students experience a variety of instruction, they also must apply many different learning strategies in each curriculum area. In both group and individual activities, students must use evaluation strategies, communication skills, problem-solving skills, data analysis skills, and critical-thinking skills. In short, *A Literature Guide to **Harry Potter and the Sorcerer's Stone*** is comprehensive across the curriculum in accordance with national standards.

Please see page 7 for a brief overview of the curriculum areas.

# Overview of National Standards
# and Curriculum Areas (continued)

**Following is a brief overview of the curriculum areas.**

**Language Arts**: Students will work with words while completing the vocabulary studies for each section. They will read and interpret literature through exercises which revolve around comprehension, nouns, figurative language, mood, setting, plot, character, making predictions, and more. Students will also have ample opportunities for journal writing, creative writing, summary writing, and report writing.

**Math**: Using information from the text, students must complete a graphing activity, a complex money/addition activity, and a challenging logic activity.

**Science**: Students will use scientific inquiry and process skills to learn about unusual animals (and create imaginary ones!), as well as perform a mysterious, polymer-making science experiment.

**Social Studies**: Geography lessons, map exercises, and a study of major historical events are included in the workbook.

**Technology**: Many of the activities in this workbook require research and some encourage the use of the Internet.

**Art**: Students have many opportunities to make art connections with the text from the novel. They create their own art, as well as use art from the workbook to interpret the novel.

# Using this Workbook

Students who are going to be reading *Harry Potter and the Sorcerer's Stone* will, like any other group of students, be of different ages, in different grades, and at different levels. It is our intention that this workbook be flexible so that it can accommodate many different types of students. This section suggests different ways to use the activities in this workbook, so that they are beneficial to a variety of readers. Below are suggestions for how to use the workbook pages.

**Vocabulary Words:** There are several ways to use the vocabulary words included in this workbook. We have suggested that students keep a record of the different pages on which they find the words. However, the first reading should probably be completed by students before searching for the vocabulary words, so that they do not turn their reading efforts into a word search. The enjoyment of reading should come first!
Use the vocabulary lists in any of the following ways, or make up your own challenges for students:
- Have students compare notes and see where in each chapter they found the words.
- Have a vocabulary word bee. Let students try to either spell or define the words.
- Let students take turns describing context clues that helped them figure out the definitions.
- Look up some of the words in several different dictionaries and compare the definitions.
- Compare the meanings of British words with their American or Canadian meanings.

**Optional Activities:** Each vocabulary page has optional activities, as do some of the other activity pages. If you do not want students to complete the optional activities, you may wish to cover that section of the worksheet with a sheet of paper before copying and handing out to students.

**Comprehension Questions:** The comprehension activities range from recounting simple facts and events, to thinking about character motivation, foreshadowing, or consequences. Some of the questions are difficult to answer without having the text in hand. Especially for younger readers, we suggest that students have the opportunity to answer the questions in open-book format, because the point is really that they think about and understand the book. You may wish to have students answer questions they know, turn in those answers, and then answer the other questions open-book, while you compare the answers which were turned in. This will allow you to assess who is doing the reading, who is understanding it well, and who is in need of extra help. Also, the answers left off the initial sheet will determine what facts and concepts are problematic for students.

**Other Activities:** The remaining activities in the book are largely extensions which take advantage of the interest students will have in the magical world created by J. K. Rowling. Some activities lend themselves to group projects, while others are more suited for individual completion. However, you should modify the activities in any way which best suits your students.

Note that on pages 13 and 49, students are required to make predictions about the text. Since many of your students may have already read *Harry Potter and the Sorcerer's Stone*, as well as other books in the series, or may have completed the comprehension questions in the beginning of each workbook section, you may want to modify these activities. Consider having students complete page 13 before they complete pages 10-11. If students have completed most or all of the series, let them predict what will happen beyond what they have read, instead of the exercise on page 49.

**Final Assessment:** Open-ended questions round out the fact-finding focus of the comprehension questions. They can be used as an exam, but it may be more effective, depending on your students, to use these questions for journal entries and class discussion starters.

# Journal Options

While we certainly permit copies of this literature guide to be made for students in your classroom, we purposefully did not include a lot of writing space on most pages in this workbook. Although teachers often find reproducible worksheets very convenient, it is suggested that each student create a React/Respond Journal (adding the reproducible pages to it) which can be used to reflect, make predictions, create stories, and respond to all of the activities in this workbook. Students will be able to keep their work organized, and they can be far more creative in making their own spaces for writing. Plus, you may find that students are inspired to do even more writing on their own!

# How to Make a Journal

Below are some suggestions for creative, inexpensive, and fun ways to create special journals for this assignment.

- A 3-ring binder or file folder is a convenient way to store loose reproducibles and journal pages. You may also want to let students have the option of storing a smaller, more "diary-like" journal in a pocket of the binder or folder.

- Create a journal with a "wizardy" flare! Have students search the school grounds for the perfect "wand." (See *Harry Potter and the Sorcerer's Stone*, Chapter Five, "Diagon Alley".) A "wand" should consist of a relatively straight tree branch, about the diameter of a pencil and at least 11" long. Stack together between 50 and 100 loose-leaf pages for a student journal. Thread a long rubber band through the top and bottom holes, with each end of the rubber band sticking out of the front, then slide the "wand" through the loops.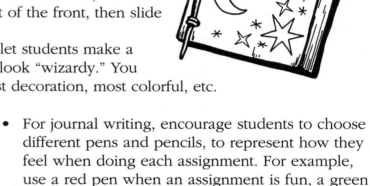

- If you are binding loose pages together, let students make a cover. If desired, they can decorate it to look "wizardy." You may even want to give prizes for the best decoration, most colorful, etc.

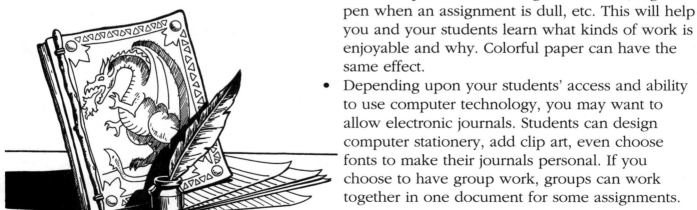

- For journal writing, encourage students to choose different pens and pencils, to represent how they feel when doing each assignment. For example, use a red pen when an assignment is fun, a green pen when an assignment is dull, etc. This will help you and your students learn what kinds of work is enjoyable and why. Colorful paper can have the same effect.

- Depending upon your students' access and ability to use computer technology, you may want to allow electronic journals. Students can design computer stationery, add clip art, even choose fonts to make their journals personal. If you choose to have group work, groups can work together in one document for some assignments.

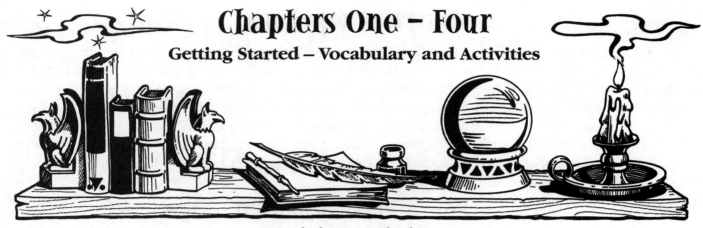

# Chapters One – Four

## Getting Started – Vocabulary and Activities

## Find the Vocabulary

To help you find the words again, write the page number where you find each vocabulary word in the space next to it. Look up any words you don't know, and write their definitions in your journal.

| | | | | |
|---|---|---|---|---|
| ___ tawny | ___ tantrum | ___ chortled | ___ peculiar | ___ enraged |
| ___ pursed | ___ quiver | ___ rummaging | ___ faltered | ___ cupboard |
| ___ frantically | ___ hoodlums | ___ specimen | ___ deafening | ___ gibber |
| ___ knickerbockers | ___ knobbly | ___ parchment | ___ wheezed | ___ trodden |
| ___ tufts | ___ bewildered | ___ quailed | ___ headmaster | ___ rubbish |
| ___ gargoyles | ___ trances | ___ ruefully | ___ gamekeeper | ___ dormice |

## Additional Activities

**React/Respond Journal**: Create a React/Respond Journal that you will use to complete all of your Harry Potter assignments. You can use any type of notebook or journal throughout this workbook for vocabulary words and other activities. Often, you will be asked to react or respond to a specific section of the book. Take some time to decorate your journal to make it both personal and fun!

**Vocabulary Fun**: You may use the vocabulary words to have a Vocabulary Bee. Choose a partner or a team, and call out words for classmates to spell and define.

**Picture It!**: In your journal, list four objects pictured on the cover of *Harry Potter and the Sorcerer's Stone*. Write what you think each object is and in what context it will appear in the book.

# Chapters One – Four
## What Do You Know? – Comprehension

### Answer the following questions in your journal.

**Chapter One: The Boy Who Lived**

1. Who are the Dursleys and where do they live?

2. What unusual things does Mr. Dursley notice one day in London?

3. Who arrives on Privet Drive disguised as a cat?

4. Why is Dumbledore on Privet Drive?

5. What form of transportation does Hagrid use to bring Harry Potter to Privet Drive, and where does he get it?

6. What do Hagrid, Professor Dumbledore, and Professor McGonagall discuss?

**Chapter Two: The Vanishing Glass**

7. The Dursleys warn Harry about causing "funny business" at the zoo. What events happen prior to the visit to the zoo that would lead them to say this?

8. What unusual event happens at the zoo, and how is Harry involved?

9. Uncle Vernon gets very angry when Harry mentions his dream. What is Harry's dream, and what does Harry see when he tries to remember a car crash?

10. Harry hopes that some unknown relative will come and take him away. Although this never happens, Harry feels that strangers in the street seem to know him. Describe two of these encounters.

11. What unusual thing happens every time Harry tries to get a closer look at these strangers?

12. Dudley has a gang at school. Everyone knows that Dudley and his gang hate Harry. How does this affect Harry?

**Chapter Three: The Letters from No One**

13. Harry receives a letter for the first time in his life. How is this letter addressed, and what happens to prevent Harry from opening it?

14. How do Aunt Petunia and Uncle Vernon react to Harry's first letter and the ones that follow?

15. Why do you think Uncle Vernon tells Harry to move into Dudley's second bedroom?

16. When Uncle Vernon can't stop the letters from coming to the house, what does he do?

17. What changes every time Harry receives a new letter?

**Chapter Four: The Keeper of the Keys**

18. At exactly midnight in the hut on the rock, something happens. What is it?

19. Hagrid appears to possess magical powers. Give three reasons for this assumption.

20. Why does Hagrid refer to the Dursleys as "Muggles?"

21. Why is Harry famous in the wizard world?

22. Why did Hagrid pull a live owl out of his pocket in Chapter Four, and what did the owl do?

23. Who is Voldemort, and why are wizards afraid of him?

24. Who is sending Harry the letters? Why?

25. Harry doesn't believe that he is a wizard. What does Hagrid say that changes Harry's mind?

# Chapter One: The Boy Who Lived
## What a Day! – Sequence of Events

Many important events happen in Chapter One of *Harry Potter and the Sorcerer's Stone*. The events happen quickly, as well. These events set up the plot for the rest of the book.

To better understand a story, it helps to be aware of the sequence of events. The **sequence of events** is the order in which events happen in a story.

**In your journal, complete the time line exercises below.**

1. In Chapter One, Mr. Dursley has quite an unusual day. Understanding the sequence of events here will help you understand what happens to Harry later in the story. In your journal, create a time line for Mr. Dursley's day as explained in the book. You can add pictures or words to the time line to explain the unusual events that occurred that day.

2. In your journal, complete the time line below for a typical weekday in your life. Share your day with a small group or with the class. Notice that except for school, most schedules are different. Share your time lines with others. Compare and contrast the events that each group included.

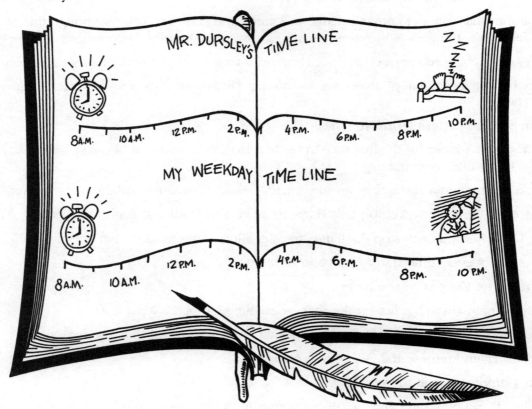

**Optional Activity:** What do you think the unusual events that happened to Mr. Dursley might mean? Write a response in your journal.

# Chapter One: The Boy Who Lived
## Who Is Harry Potter? – Making Predictions

In Chapter One, J. K. Rowling introduces many characters. Only at the very end of the chapter do we meet Harry Potter.

When we analyze or study characters in a story, we can **make predictions** about the characters and the events in the story. It is often fun to make predictions and then compare our theories or ideas to the actual events as the story unfolds.

### Predict the future.

Answer the following questions using information you know about the Dursleys. Write the answers in your journal.

1. What is the Dursleys' secret?

2. Why does Mrs. Dursley dislike her sister?

3. Who are the odd-looking people dressed in cloaks?

4. Why are there so many owls flying overhead?

5. Who is "You Know Who"/Voldemort?

6. What is a Muggle?

7. Why is it "raining" shooting stars?

8. Who is Albus Dumbledore?

9. What is everyone celebrating?

10. What kind of world does Harry Potter come from?

11. Who is Harry Potter, and why is he famous?

12. Where did Harry get the lightning-shaped scar on his forehead?

13. Who is Sirius Black?

14. Will Harry have a good life with the Dursleys?

15. Will Harry and his cousin Dudley become good friends?

16. Will Harry ever know why he is famous? How?

# Chapter Two: The Vanishing Glass
## Give Me Reasons! – Cause and Effect

By this point in the story, we know *something* has happened (**cause**) that forced Hagrid to leave Harry on his aunt and uncle's doorstep (**effect**). To comprehend a story more clearly, it is important to realize *why* things happen. The events in a story can be organized and understood by cause and effect. The **cause** is the reason why something happens and the **effect** is the result, or what happens. Sometimes, you may not be able to determine the cause and effect until you read more of the book.

**Fill in either the missing cause or effect.**

| | Cause | Effect |
|---|---|---|
| 1. | | *Harry is used to spiders.* |
| 2. | The only clothes Harry owned were Dudley's old clothes that were about four sizes too big for him. | |
| 3. | | *Dudley is on the verge of a tantrum.* |
| 4. | Mrs. Figgs phones to say she has broken her leg, and can't watch Harry. | |
| 5. | | *Aunt Petunia cuts Harry's hair very short, leaving only bangs to hide his scar.* |
| 6. | | *Harry ends up sitting on the chimney.* |
| 7. | Harry thinks the boa constrictor must be bored living in one tank all its life. | |
| 8. | Uncle Vernon is very angry with Harry after the snake incident. | |
| 9. | | *Harry has no friends in school.* |

# Chapter Two: The Vanishing Glass
## Can You See It? – Descriptive Paragraphs

In Chapter Two, J. K. Rowling describes Harry's life with the Dursleys. From these descriptions, the author expects you to form an opinion about what life is like for Harry.

A **descriptive paragraph** describes something, such as a person, a place, a thing, or an idea. A descriptive paragraph should allow the reader to see, hear, smell, taste and feel the things you are describing. Good descriptions help readers imagine what it is like to be in the story.

**Describe life with the Dursleys.**

1. In your journal, write down the descriptions of the life Harry is living. Then, use your own ideas to write a descriptive paragraph in your journal about Harry's life with the Dursleys.

2. Think about what you have learned about Harry's life. Is it pleasant? Is it the same as yours, or different? Find a few descriptions in the book that support what you think. In your paragraph, remember to include an interesting **topic sentence**, which states the main idea. For example, if you think Harry's life with the Dursleys is exciting, that could be your topic sentence. Then, find descriptions, and talk about them in **supporting sentences**. These sentences will show why you have formed your opinion. Finally, include a **closing sentence**, which summarizes what you have discussed in your paragraph.

# Chapter Three: The Letters from No One
## Room for Debate! – Public Speaking

Harry receives numerous letters in Chapter Three. Although the address changes as Harry relocates, the letters are always addressed to him. It is apparent from Uncle Vernon's reaction to the letters that he is aware of the identity of the sender, and as Harry's guardian, has chosen not to allow Harry to read them. Harry insists that he has a right to read the letters since they are addressed to him, but Uncle Vernon disagrees. Uncle Vernon insists that since he is Harry's guardian, he has a right to raise Harry as he sees fit. Do you support Harry or Uncle Vernon on this issue?

A **debate** is a contest in which two opposing sides of a position are argued by two or more speakers.

### Have a debate.

1. **Form debate teams** of 4-5 people.

2. **Make a position statement.** Your statement will tell if you will be arguing that Harry should or should not be allowed to read the letters. Remember, you may have to argue the position with which you disagree.

3. **Research the issue.** With your team, look for places in the text which support your position. Be prepared to quote them during the debate. Also, think of other places you can research to help your argument. For example, what are the laws which decide who gets to read mail? What are the laws determining the responsibilities of guardianship? Do these laws apply to England as well as to the United States?

4. **Brainstorm** with your team to identify your prime arguments (you need 3-4). Agree as a team to their significance and importance.

5. **List** your arguments in descending order of importance. In other words, list the most important argument first, the next-most-important argument second, etc. Prepare a **conclusion**, which summarizes the important points.

6. **Select** a member of your team whom you feel will best present your arguments and state your team's conclusion. He or she will have five minutes to present, so help the presenter practice the debate. Use a watch or timer to ensure the time limit is met.

7. **Extend** your debate by including a question-and-answer session. Give each member on both teams an opportunity to ask one question of an opposing team member. Limit answers to one minute.

8. **Conclude** your debate and determine a winner. Let the audience of the debate vote on the winner, then give feedback as to why the winning team was more persuasive.

### Optional Activities:
1. Write a letter to Harry or Uncle Vernon persuading them to see your position on the issue.

2. Determine other important classroom or school issues which could be debated.

# Chapter Three: The Letters from No One
## Changes for the Dursleys – Character Analysis

In Chapters One and Two, Uncle Vernon, Aunt Petunia, and Dudley treat Harry more like a servant than a nephew. Although Aunt Petunia feeds him, he is never really satisfied, and things like treats and new clothes are never given to Harry. Even Dudley, who is his cousin, never shares his toys or includes Harry in any fun activities. On the contrary, Dudley seems to do everything in his power to make Harry's life more miserable than it already is. Then one day, Harry receives a letter in the mail. Actually, he receives hundreds of letters, and they don't arrive like normal letters at all! Throughout this chapter, as Harry is receiving the letters, we see changes in the Dursleys' attitudes toward Harry. What are those changes and why do they occur?

**Use the following graphic organizer to help you analyze and understand these changes in the characters' behavior.**

### Beginning of the Chapter

1.

| Character | Attitude toward Harry | Example to support your statement |
|---|---|---|
| Uncle Vernon | | |
| Aunt Petunia | | |
| Dudley | | |

### Middle of the Chapter

2.

| Character | Attitude toward Harry | Example to support your statement |
|---|---|---|
| Uncle Vernon | | |
| Aunt Petunia | | |
| Dudley | | |

### End of the Chapter

3.

| Character | Attitude toward Harry | Example to support your statement |
|---|---|---|
| Uncle Vernon | | |
| Aunt Petunia | | |
| Dudley | | |

**Optional Activity:** If you were in Harry's situation and had to live with relatives who at first treated you poorly, then changed their attitudes toward you, how would you feel? How would you react? Use your React/Respond Journal to answer these questions.

# Chapter Four: Keeper of the Keys
## Be Wise as an Owl! – Similes

In Chapter Four, as in the rest of the book, J. K. Rowling uses many similes to help describe things vividly. Authors often use similes when writing to help readers form pictures in their minds. A **simile** is a comparison of two unlike things that have something in common. Similes use the words **like** or **as** to join the two parts of a sentence. For example: His magic potion smelled **like** a skunk.

**With a partner, reread Chapter Four and search for similes. Remember to look for *comparisons* that use like or as. Write down each simile (and the page number) as you find it. Give yourself one tally mark for every simile you find!**

| | Tally Mark | Simile |
|---|---|---|
| 1. | ✔ | |
| 2. | | |
| 3. | | |
| 4. | | |
| 5. | | |
| 6. | | |
| 7. | | |
| 8. | | |
| 9. | | |
| 10. | | |

 = Total of tally marks

## Total Score
1 – 3 Look again. Finding similes can be like looking for a needle in a haystack!
4 – 7 Keep searching. Your skill at finding similes will improve as fast as lightning!
7 – 10 You are as clever as a wizard!

**Optional Activity**: Use your React/Respond Journal to write your own similes to describe some of the main characters introduced thus far. Share them with your classmates.

# Chapter Four: Keeper of the Keys
## What Is Harry's Story? – Writing a Summary

In Chapter Four we finally learn about Harry's past. Hagrid explains to Harry who he is, and about the world his parents knew. To tell this to Harry quickly, Hagrid has to **summarize** a lot of events. Hagrid tells Harry the main things that happened, but not all of the details.

A summary should include the most important ideas in a story or chapter. You should put those ideas together in logical order to write a clear and simple mini-report. Write our own summary about Harry's past. Be sure to include the world he came from, his parents and what happened to them, and of course, Harry, and why he is famous in his world.

**Use the following writing process guide to help you write a good summary. Refer to page 45 for additional help with the steps in the writing process.**

**Prewriting** (This is the planning stage. Do this before you write your summary.)
- Read the selection carefully.
- Skim through it a second time, making a list of important ideas or events.
- Share your list with a partner to make sure you have not missed anything.
- Make sure your ideas are in logical order. If not, number them to make writing easier.

**Writing Your First Draft**
- Your first sentence should be the topic sentence, which states the main idea of your summary.
- Remember to include only the most important information. Do not include many details.
- Add a concluding sentence if you think one is necessary for your summary. (You will have to have a concluding sentence in a report, of course.)

**Revising** (This is a very important step in which you should change ideas, add/remove sentences, and evaluate your word choices.)
- Read your summary over carefully to see if all your important ideas are included.
- Check to make sure you used your own words, and use quotations marks and citations for any text that you quoted.
- Check to make sure your sentences are interesting, and that the summary you have written is thorough and doesn't leave out any major events.

**Editing** (At this stage, check carefully for errors, and have a dictionary handy!)
- Check for spelling and punctuation errors.
- Trade papers with an editing partner.

**Preparing a Final Draft**
- Write the final draft of your summary in your best handwriting.

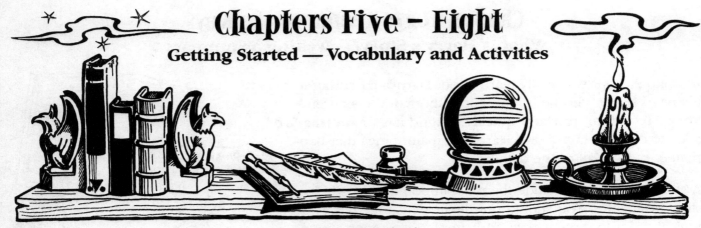

# Chapters Five – Eight
## Getting Started — Vocabulary and Activities

## Find the Vocabulary

To help you find the words again, write the page number where you find each vocabulary word in the space next to it. Look up any words you don't know, and write their definitions in your journal.

___ collapsed          ___ savaging          ___ enchantments   ___ vaults          ___ clambered

___ transfiguration    ___ cauldron          ___ bloke          ___ hag             ___ Apothecary

___ prickled           ___ gawking           ___ ruddy          ___ jostled         ___ corridor

___ astonishment       ___ wailed            ___ stunned        ___ dumbfounded     ___ riffraff

___ drone              ___ chamber           ___ dormitory      ___ toil            ___ sallow

___ poltergeist        ___ subtle            ___ ensnaring      ___ bewitching      ___ crossbow

## Additional Activities

**The Card Game:** In groups, divide the vocabulary words evenly. On index cards, write a vocabulary word on one side and the definition on the other side. Use your cards to quiz other groups.

**Puzzle Fun:** Using graph paper, create a word search with your vocabulary words. Exchange papers with a classmate.

**Sentence Work:** Use each vocabulary word in a sentence, using it in the same way it is used in the book. Identify the part of speech of each vocabulary word.

# Chapters Five – Eight
## What Do You Know? – Comprehension

### Answer the following questions in your journal.

**Chapter Five: Diagon Alley**

1. How does Hagrid get to the hut on the rocks, and then speed up his and Harry's trip to London?

2. What is Gringotts? Where is it? Who runs it? Why is it a safe place for wizards?

3. Who is the Minister of Magic? What is his main job, and why is it an important job?

4. What is so curious about the wand that chooses Harry at Mr. Ollivander's shop?

5. Why does Mr. Ollivander, the wand shopkeeper, expect "great things" from Harry, based upon the wand that chooses Harry?

6. When is Harry to report to Hogwarts, and how is he supposed to get there?

**Chapter Six: The Journey from Platform Nine and Three-Quarters**

7. How does Harry get onto the correct platform at the train station?

8. Who does Harry meet at the train station and on the train? How does everyone know Harry's identity?

9. Ginny Weasley's brothers promise her "loads of owls." What does this really mean?

10. Name the characters on the Chocolate Frog cards that Harry opens.

11. According to a Chocolate Frog card, who is Dumbledore? What did he do? Who is his partner?

12. What clues in Chapter Six let you know that the story takes place in the present time?

13. What does Ron Weasley tell Harry about Draco Malfoy's family?

**Chapter Seven: The Sorting Hat**

14. What is a Sorting Ceremony, and what special powers does the sorting hat possess?

15. Name the four houses at Hogwarts. Identify the qualities associated with each house on which a student's placement is based.

16. What events in Chapter Seven lead you to believe that magical things happen at Hogwarts?

17. How does the banquet begin on Harry's first night at Hogwarts? What did the students get to eat?

18. What two locations are off-limits to the students at Hogwarts? Why?

**Chapter Eight: The Potions Master**

19. How many staircases are there at Hogwarts? How are they different from staircases in a normal building?

20. What is unusual about the portraits in the corridors and the doors at Hogwarts?

21. What does the following statement mean? "Peeves the Poltergeist was worth two locked doors and a trick staircase if you met him when you were late for class."

22. Professor Snape promises to teach the students things if they are not "dunderheads." What does he promise to teach them, and what do you think his promises mean?

23. How does Harry lose two points for Gryffindor during his first week at Hogwarts? How do you think he feels?

24. Why does Harry think Professor Snape hates him?

25. Why is Harry so interested in the break-in at Gringotts?

# Chapter Five: Diagon Alley
## What's in Harry's Trunk? – Graphing

Harry goes shopping with Hagrid in Diagon Alley to purchase supplies that he will need for school at Hogwarts. Harry's trunk is so heavy that when he finally boards the train to travel to Hogwarts, it takes three people to lift his trunk off the platform.

**Follow the directions below to find out why Harry's trunk was so heavy.**

1. In a small group, read through Chapter Five, and list all of the items Harry buys. Place each item into one of these four categories: books, clothing, equipment, or animals.

2. Now, make a fraction for each category, to show what percentage of Harry's purchases each item represents. For example, if Harry bought 6 total items, and 2 of those were books, the fraction would be $\frac{2}{6}$ or $\frac{1}{3}$. Therefore, that $\frac{1}{3}$ of the items Harry purchased were books.

3. Next, make a large circle, which you will turn into a **pie chart**. Divide it into the same number of sections as there are items purchased. For example, if Harry only bought six different items, you would divide the circle like the one at right, with one section for each item.

4. Decide on a **color key**. You could choose gray to represent books, red to represent clothing, etc. Then, color one section in the pie chart for each item of that type. Using the example from number 2, you would color the books section of the pie chart like the one at right (one section for each book, making $\frac{1}{3}$ of the circle gray).

5. Answer these questions in your journal: Which type of item took up the largest percentage of space in the trunk? How would this affect the weight of the trunk? Which item would not be packed in the trunk? Why not?

# Chapter Five: Diagon Alley
## How Much Is It? – Math Connection

Harry has had no money to spend for most of his life. In addition, Aunt Petunia and Uncle Vernon frequently complain that caring for Harry costs them too much money. When Hagrid takes Harry to Gringotts, the bank for witches and wizards, Harry is amazed to learn that he has a vault full of money. Although he has yet to learn their value, he stuffs his pockets with gold Galleons, silver Sickles, and bronze Knuts in order to purchase his school supplies.

**Help Harry solve the problems below to become a whiz at wizard money.**

**29 Knuts = 1 Sickle      17 Sickles = 1 Galleon**

1.  Harry paid 7 gold Galleons for his magic wand. How many Sickles would he need to use?

2.  If Harry purchased a telescope for 2 Galleons, glass phials for 493 Knuts, a set of brass scales for 3 Galleons, and an owl for 51 Sickles, how much did he spend in Knuts?
    In Sickles?   In Galleons?

3.  How many Knuts are equivalent to 1 Galleon?

4.  What is the equivalent of 1,479 Knuts in Sickles?
    In Galleons?

5.  Harry purchased the following wardrobe:
    Three plain work robes cost 102 Sickles (total for all three).
    One plain pointed hat cost 17 Sickles.
    A pair of protective gloves cost 17 Sickles.
    One winter cloak cost 51 Sickles.
    How many Sickles did he use to make his purchase?
    Harry discovers he is out of Sickles and decides to use
    Galleons. How many Galleons must he use for the same purchase?

6.  Harry purchases the book *One Thousand Magical Herbs and Fungi* on sale. It originally cost 3 Galleons. The discount is 17 Sickles. How much does the book cost now in Galleons?

7.  *Magical Drafts and Potions, Fantastic Beasts and Where to Find Them* and *The Dark Forces* cost a total of 21 Galleons. *Dark Forces* costs twice as much as *Fantastic Beasts and Where to Find Them. Magical Drafts and Potions* costs 1 Galleon more then *Fantastic Beasts and Where to Find Them.* What is the cost of each book?

8.  Harry begins his shopping spree with a total of 45 Galleons, 34 Sickles and 1,479 Knuts. How much wizard money does Harry have in Galleons?   In Sickles?   In Knuts?

# Chapter Six: The Journey from Platform Nine and Three-Quarters
## Where Is Harry Potter? – Geography Connection

In Chapter Six, Harry takes the Hogwarts Express train to Hogwarts School. The train passes cow pastures, woods, winding rivers, dark green hills, and reaches a forest and high mountains. However, the text never reveals the part of the country in which Hogwarts is located.

**Use a map of the United Kingdom to label and complete the map above.**

1. Identify and outline England, Scotland, and Wales. Draw the island of Ireland, which is also part of the United Kingdom. Locate the following major cities on the map and write them next to the small squares.

   | London | Manchester | Liverpool | Edinburgh | Glasgow | Birmingham |

2. Identify the major mountain ranges and rivers in England, and the surrounding oceans. Label them on the map.

   **Severn River** **Thames River** **Ouse River** **Trent River** **Grampian Mountains**
   **Forth River** **North Sea** **Atlantic Ocean** **Irish Sea** **Cambrian Mountains**

3. In your journal, research the following information about the United Kingdom. Write the answers in your journal.

   Area     Population     Capital     Largest City     Highest Point

4. Reread the sections in the novel which describe Harry's trip. Harry's trip begins at 11:00 a.m. and ends sometime in the early evening. Using the information about the scenery and the amount of time Harry travels, consult an atlas and determine possible locations for Hogwarts. Use the map to assist you in your search. Draw a wizard's hat on the spot you believe Hogwarts to be. Use your React/Respond Journal to explain your reasoning.

# Chapter Six: The Journey from Platform Nine and Three-Quarters
## Where Will Harry Live? – Setting

As Harry's train approaches Hogwarts, the author begins to describe the school and the area surrounding it. The **setting** describes the time and place of a story. It also identifies objects in the story (for example: many turrets, great black lake, starry sky).

**Following the directions below, work first as a team, then alone, and finally, as a team again, to create a mysterious, magical mural of Hogwarts.**

1. **First**, in small groups, skim through Chapter Six to identify the descriptive words and phrases the author uses to describe this mysterious new world. In your mind, try to picture the setting of Hogwarts. List the descriptive words and phrases on the lines below.

_____

_____

_____

_____

_____

_____

_____

_____

_____

_____

2. **Next**, using your own imagination and knowledge of castles, draw Hogwarts in its surroundings as Harry first views it upon his arrival.

3. **Then**, compare your drawing with the drawings of your group members. Evaluate them based upon your list of descriptive phrases.

4. **Finally**, as a team, choose the best details of each drawing and together create a mural, or artistic scene, of Hogwarts, Harry's new home.

# Chapter Seven - The Sorting Hat
## Who Are the Teachers? – Making Predictions

While Harry attends the banquet after the Sorting Ceremony, he sees several of the teachers from a distance. Some have been mentioned earlier, and Harry has met Professor Quirrell, but Harry gets a chance to study them and, perhaps, wonder what all the teachers are like. He doesn't know what all of them are teaching, but he gets an idea of what their personalities might be. Sometimes he gets clues from their appearances, and sometimes from their behaviors. Sometimes first impressions prove to be accurate, and sometimes they do not.

**Use Harry's first impressions to make predictions about the teachers.**

On the lines provided, write the first few things the text says about each Professor listed below. Then, from what Harry is thinking, predict what you think each teacher listed below will be like. Write your predictions in your journal.

1. Professor McGonagall _____

   _____

   _____

2. Professor Dumbledore _____

   _____

   _____

3. Professor Quirrell _____

   _____

   _____

4. Professor Snape _____

   _____

   _____

**Optional Activity**: With the exception of Dumbledore, these and others will be Harry's teachers for the next year. What do you think are good qualities for a teacher to have? Which of these teachers do you think will have those qualities, and why? Write a paragraph about your answers in your journal.

# Chapter Seven - The Sorting Hat
## Whose House Is It? – Classification Skills

In Chapter Seven, Harry and his new friend, Ron, are very nervous about being sorted into one of the four houses at Hogwarts. Although Harry is relieved to learn he does not have to perform any phenomenal feats, he is still concerned because at the moment, he doesn't exactly "feel brave or quick-witted." There are four houses at Hogwarts. The sorting hat uses **classification** to assign to a house for specific reasons.

### Use classification skills to complete the activities below.

To help you better understand each new character, follow the directions below to create a chart, which you can add to, as you meet new characters in the remaining chapters. Remember, only "first years" are sorted at the ceremony. There are many other, older students who need to be added to your chart.

1. Create a chart, similar to the one shown at right, with four columns. Label each column using the name of the four houses at Hogwarts. Under the name of each house, write the personality and character traits of each house.

| Hufflepuff | Gryffindor | Ravenclaw | Slytherin |
|---|---|---|---|
| ____ | ____ | ____ | ____ |
| ____ | ____ | ____ | ____ |
| ____ | ____ | ____ | ____ |
|  |  |  |  |

2. Sort the students according to the sorting hat's choices. Add older students if you know in which house they belong. If you do not have a house name for certain students, put their names on a separate list and look for their houses as you read the book. You can also add the names of the professors and ghosts assigned to each house.

3. If you were at Hogwarts, where would the sorting hat place you? Be honest. Think about aspects of your personality, then explain why you chose that house. Who do you think could be your friends at Hogwarts? Could your friends come from other houses? Use your React/Respond Journal to answer these questions. Then, compare notes with the rest of your class and see where everyone is sorted!

# Chapter Eight: The Potions Master
## Name This! – Proper Nouns

As Harry starts classes in Chapter Eight, we are introduced to many new classes and people. A **common noun** names a person, place, or thing and begins with a lowercase letter. Some examples are state, statue, and boy. A **proper noun** names a specific person, place, or thing and always begins with a capital letter. Proper nouns can be made up of one or more words and both must be capitalized. Small words, in the middle of proper nouns, like *a, of, an,* or *the* do not need a capital letter. Some examples are New Jersey, the Statue of Liberty, and the name Ron.

### Complete the search for proper nouns.

Search through Chapter Eight and identify all the proper nouns. List them in the chart below. Then, on the back of this paper, choose fifteen proper nouns, and use them to write fifteen sentences. Make sure your sentences contain factual information that relates to the context of the story, to help you remember new information. For example, if you chose the proper noun *Herbology*, your sentence could be, "Herbology is the class in which Harry learns about magical plants." **Note:** Ghosts are considered people for this exercise.

## Proper Nouns in Chapter Eight

| People | Places | Things |
|---|---|---|
|  |  |  |

**How did you do?** Did you find all fifty-two proper nouns?
Give yourself fifty-one Hogwarts points if you did!

# Chapter Eight: The Potions Master
## Who Teaches What? – Character Study

In Chapter Eight, J. K. Rowling introduces us to some very interesting characters—Harry's teachers. Now's your chance to get to know the professors and the classes they teach. Pay attention—what you learn now might be important later!

**Draw a line to match each professor to the class he or she teaches.**

| | |
|---|---|
| Professor Snape | Herbology |
| Professor Binns | Potions |
| Professor Flitwick | Defense Against the Dark Arts |
| Professor McGonagall | History of Magic |
| Professor Sprout | Charms |
| Professor Quirrell | Transfiguration |

**Answer the following questions in your journal.**

1. Which class would you be in if you were taking notes about great wizards of the past century?

2. If you rubbed against an odd-looking plant and started to get green bumps on your body, which professor would be able to help you?

3. In which class would you need to use your cauldron, crystal phials, and brass scales?

4. Which class would you be in if you were taller than the professor?

5. If you made a mistake mixing ingredients for an elixir of warmth, which professor would take house points away from you?

6. If you only changed half of your quill pen into a mouse, and ended up with a two-legged mouse with a feather for a back end, in which class would you be?

**Optional Activities**: In your React/Respond Journal, answer the following questions. Discuss the results with others.

1. Which professor do you like the most? Why?
2. In which class would you most like to be? Why?
3. If you could be a professor, what subject would you teach? Why?

# Chapters Nine – Twelve
## Getting Started – Vocabulary and Activities

### Find the Vocabulary

To help you find the words again, write the page number where you find each vocabulary word in the space next to it. Look up any words you don't know, and write their definitions in your journal.

| | | | | |
|---|---|---|---|---|
| ___ boastful | ___ extraordinary | ___ quaver | ___ javelin | ___ triumphant |
| ___ looming | ___ embers | ___ hurtled | ___ bellowed | ___ snarled |
| ___ impatient | ___ griffin | ___ waggled | ___ slouched | ___ echoes |
| ___ berserk | ___ flailed | ___ championship | ___ conjured | ___ mangled |
| ___ diversion | ___ jinxing | ___ brandished | ___ askew | ___ chipolatas |
| ___ crackers | ___ crumpets | ___ eerie | ___ earsplitting | ___ inscription |

### Additional Activities

**Play Charades**: Choose teams. Have one member of each team choose a vocabulary word from a hat and attempt to act it out. You can set a time limit of sixty seconds for each word to keep the game moving.

**Puzzle Fun:** Use your vocabulary words to create a crossword puzzle.

**Acrostic Poems**: Choose one vocabulary word and create an acrostic poem related to the word.

**Example:**  **Q**uite a cool writing pen
**U**sed in Colonial America
**I**s used with ink
**L**ooks like a feather
**L**oads of fun to use!

# Chapters Nine – Twelve
## What Do You Know? – Comprehension

### Answer the following questions in your journal.

**Chapter Nine: The Midnight Duel**

1.  What is a Remembrall? Who receives one and why?

2.  Why does Harry think he will be expelled from Hogwarts? What happens instead?

3.  What is a wizard's duel? Why is Hermione upset with Harry for agreeing to one?

4.  Draco Malfoy does not meet Harry for the wizard's duel. Describe the events when Harry arrives at the trophy room on the third floor.

5.  What does Harry mean when he thinks that he has "walked into a nightmare?"

6.  Describe the monstrous dog in the forbidden corridor on the third floor. What does Harry think it is protecting?

**Chapter Ten: Halloween**

7.  What does Harry receive by owl messenger that makes him extremely happy and Draco Malfoy jealous?

8.  What is Quidditch? Who are the members on the team, and what do they do?

9.  Why is so important for Wood to explain the game of Quidditch to Harry before they started practicing?

10.  Why is everyone sent back to their dormitories during the Halloween festivities?

11.  Who defeats the troll and how? Why is Professor McGonagall angry with Harry and his friends?

12.  Why do Harry and Ron befriend Hermione?

**Chapter Eleven: Quidditch**

13.  What facts does Harry learn about Quidditch by reading the book Hermione gives him?

14.  What does Harry figure out about how Snape hurt his leg? Why doesn't Hermione agree?

15.  Why is Dean Thomas yelling at the referee during the Quidditch game to "Send him off...Red card!" when Harry is fouled?

16.  Who was Fluffy, and where did Hagrid get him?

17.  How does Professor Flitwick decorate the last Christmas tree after Hagrid brings it to the Great Hall?

18.  Does Hagrid believe that Snape is trying to harm Harry? What is his explanation?

**Chapter Twelve: The Mirror of Erised**

19.  Why are the Weasley children staying at Hogwarts for Christmas?

20.  How many presents does Harry receive for his first Christmas at Hogwarts? What does he receive, and who sends them?

21.  What is the special gift Harry receives? Who do you think sends it? Why?

22.  What are wizard crackers, and what does Harry receive in his at the Christmas feast?

23.  For what purpose does Harry use his invisibility cloak the first time he wears it?

24.  How does the Mirror of Erised work? What do Harry and Ron see in the mirror? Why?

25.  What is Dumbledore's advice to Harry about the mirror?

# Chapter Nine: The Midnight Duel
## Be an Inventor – Poetry Connection

In Chapter Nine, a barn owl delivers a package to Neville Longbottom. When he opens it, he discovers a "Remembrall." A "Remembrall" is a small glass ball that, when touched, turns red if you've forgotten to do something. Since most of us sometimes forget to do things, (sometimes even homework!), a Remembrall would be a wonderful object to own. Think of the times you were in trouble for not doing something. Were they times you honestly forgot to do something?

### Invent a gadget.

Try to invent something that would be useful to you in your everyday life. (No homework machines, please. Homework is useful!) It can have magical powers like the "Remembrall." Be creative! Think about what you do every day and what would make your life easier.

### Write a poem.

After you've decided what to invent, explain it in a poem. Any type of poetry is acceptable. Be sure to explain in detail how to use your invention, and what it does for you. Write your final copy in your journal. Add a diagram of your invention to show how it works. To help you along, below are two examples of traditional poetry.

**Ballad**: This type of poem tells a story. Each stanza has four lines. Many times the second and fourth lines rhyme.

> Once again I forgot to do
> The chores my grandma had given me.
> Now she's mad, and I am sad.
> She calls me "Neville Forgetful," you see.
>
> But one day I got a Remembrall
> A barn owl brought it through the door.
> It magically turns red and won't let me forget
> To do my chores and much, much more!

**Limerick**: This is a short, humorous poem with five lines. The line scheme is *aabba* (lines one, two, and five rhyme while lines three and four do also). There are three stressed syllables lines in one, two and five, and two stressed syllables in lines three and four. [Stressed syllables (in bold) are emphasized when reading the poem.]

> There **once** was a **boy** named **Ne**ville
> Who was **of**ten **ve**ry for**get**ful.
> Till his **Gran** sent a **ball**,
> With **white** smoke and **all**,
> Which was **ta**ken by **Mal**foy, that **de**vil.

# Chapter Nine: The Midnight Duel
## What Does It Mean? – Figurative Language

J. K. Rowling often uses colorful and interesting phrases that have different literal meanings from the actual words. This is called **figurative language**. One type of figurative language is called a **simile** (see page 18). Similes are phrases using *like* or *as* to compare one thing to another in order to create a vivid image. An example is: *His wand crackled and popped **like** a fire.* Another type of figurative language is called a **metaphor**. Metaphors are also comparisons, but they do not use *like* or *as*. For example: *Her temper was a monster.* Finally, **symbolism** makes an image or object stand for another. In the phrase "*It was raining cats and dogs,*" cats and dogs obviously stand for large, pelting raindrops, since we know that animals do not usually fall out of the sky.

**Below are some examples of figurative language from Chapter Nine. In your journal, write the real meanings of the phrases.**

1. "They were half hoping for a reason to fight Malfoy, but Professor McGonagall, who could spot trouble quicker than any teacher in the school, **was there in a flash**."

2. "**Neville was hanging on to her every word**, desperate for anything that might help him hang on to his broomstick later, but everybody else was very pleased when Hermione's lecture was interrupted by the arrival of the mail."

3. "This was something you couldn't **learn by heart** out of a book — not that she hadn't tried."

4. " 'Well, what are you all waiting for?' **she barked**."

5. " 'Come back, boy!' she shouted, but **Neville was rising straight up like a cork shot out of a bottle** — twelve feet — twenty feet."

6. "For a moment, he was sure **he'd walked into a nightmare** — this was too much, on top of everything that had happened so far."

7. " '—a century,' said Harry, **shoveling pie into his mouth**."

8. "The crystal trophy cases glimmered where the **moonlight caught them.**"

**Optional Activity**: In your groups, think of other examples of figurative language. Then, choose one sentence and illustrate the phrase both literally (word for word) and figuratively (the actual meaning).

# Chapter Ten: Halloween
## How Do They Feel? – Mood

J. K. Rowling takes us on a whirlwind of emotions throughout *Harry Potter and the Sorcerer's Stone*, and the overall mood may be described in many ways. There are times when it is bittersweet (both happy and sad at once), suspenseful, mysterious, or amusing. Readers turn each page and feel something different. In Chapter Ten, Harry and his friends experience many mood changes for us to explore.

The **mood** of a book is the overall feeling a reader gets while reading. Mood usually changes throughout the story. Authors create a mood by using descriptive words that make the reader feel a certain way. The story setting and story events also help develop mood.

 **Look for mood indicators.**

Use the chart below to describe the mood in this chapter. Look for adjectives the author uses to help create the mood. Remember that an **adjective** is a describing word (a word that modifies a noun or a pronoun).

| | Event | Feelings associated with the event | Adjectives or phrases used by the author |
|---|---|---|---|
| 1. | The day Harry receives his new broomstick. | | |
| 2. | Harry, Ron, and Hermione's battle with the troll. | | |
| 3. | The lecture they receive from Professor McGonagall. | | |
| 4. | The revelation that they are now friends forever. | | |

**Optional Activity**: Test your own writing skills. Try to create a certain mood, remembering how important adjectives are in creating the mood. Choose from the following list of moods, then write a paragraph in your journal. Finally, share your paragraph with the rest of your class.

1. Calm and peaceful 2. Tense and suspenseful 3. Mysterious 4. Happy and hopeful 5. Scary

# Chapter Ten: Halloween
## What A Game! – Compare and Contrast

In Chapter Nine, we read that, "Ron had already had a big argument with Dean Thomas, who shared their dormitory, about soccer. Ron couldn't see what was exciting about a game with only one ball where no one was allowed to fly." In Chapter Ten, Oliver Wood explains the differences between soccer and Quidditch. How many similarities and differences are there between Soccer and Quidditch?

Soccer is called "football" in countries other than the United States. The World Cup, which is an international professional soccer championship, is played once every four years. Soccer is played with eleven players who may use their feet and heads, but not their hands. The goalkeeper is the only player allowed to use his hands, but only in a designated area of the field. The equipment needed for soccer is a soccer ball and shin guards. The field is a rectangular shape approximately 50 yards by 100 yards. There are two goals, one on each end of the field. The game is played for two 45-minute periods. Overtime may be played in the event of a tied score. When the entire ball crosses the goal line between the two goal posts and under the crossbar, a goal is scored. There are penalties in soccer for being offsides, committing fouls, and misconduct. In the event of penalties, direct free kicks, indirect free kicks, and penalty kicks are awarded to the opposing team.

### Compare soccer to Quidditch.

Read through Chapter Ten, focusing on the part in which Wood arrives to teach Harry how to play Quidditch. As you read, take notes in your journal about the players, positions, equipment, playing field, duration of game, scoring, and penalties. Then, look up how to play soccer, and use the graphic organizer below to compare and contrast soccer to Quidditch.

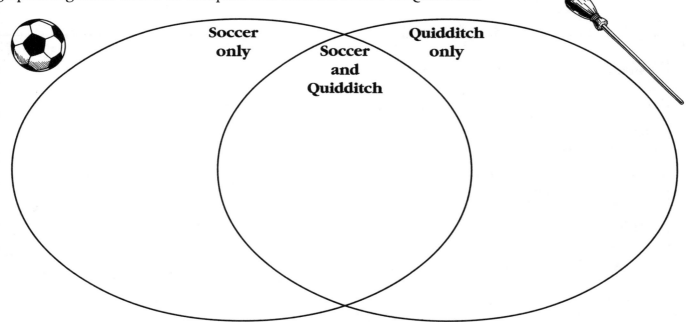

**Optional Activity**: Using the graphic organizer above for reference, draw a soccer game or a Quidditch game in action. Identify players, goals, boundaries, etc.

# Chapter Eleven: Quidditch
## It's A Mystery! – Draw Conclusions

At the end of Chapter Eleven, J. K. Rowling gives us many facts and clues that lead us to believe that something strange is going on at Hogwarts.

**Drawing conclusions** while reading is a process that readers do naturally, to better understand a story. When you draw conclusions in a story, you use facts given by the author, along with your own knowledge and experience, to make an educated guess about upcoming events in a story.

**Fill in the characters involved in each incident and make a decision about the outcome.**

| | Event | Characters | Possible Conclusion |
|---|---|---|---|
| 1. | Vault 713 is emptied of a "grubby little package wrapped up in brown paper." | *Hagrid, Harry, Griphook* | *Hagrid is bringing the package to Hogwarts.* |
| 2. | Students are forbidden to use the third floor of Hogwarts. | *Dumbledore* | |
| 3. | A three-headed dog is seen guarding a trapdoor. | | |
| 4. | There is a troll loose in the school. | | |
| 5. | Snape has a bad wound on his leg. | | |
| 6. | There is something wrong with Harry's new broomstick. | | |
| 7. | Hagrid mentions the name Nicolas Flamel. | | *Nicolas Flamel is involved with the secret.* |

**List any other incidents or clues in your journal.**

**Optional Activities**
1. What, if anything, is hidden and guarded at Hogwarts?
2. Is someone trying to steal it?
3. Who is Nicolas Flamel and how is he involved?
4. Is someone out to hurt Harry? If so, who, and why?

# Chapter Eleven: Quidditch
## Go Team Go! – Art Connection

In Chapter Eleven, Harry plays his first Quidditch game. The game is between the Gryffindor team and the Slytherin team. Harry is very nervous that morning and has a difficult time eating breakfast. J.K. Rowling builds a lot of suspense in readers by letting us see how nervous Harry is.

In this chapter, as well as in Chapter Ten, there are many descriptions of Quidditch. The sport turns out to be a very important part of the characters' lives. Therefore, it is important that readers understand the rules of the game and the layout of the field.

### Make your own Quidditch field!

To improve your understanding of the game of Quidditch, form small groups, then use available art supplies and supplies from nature (twigs, moss, etc.) to create a three-dimensional model of a Quidditch field. Include the goals, the balls, and the flying players. Refer to the book for the correct number of players, goals, and balls.

### Consider the following questions as you build your field.

From what materials will you make your players?

How many players are there in all?

How can you suspend your players and balls so they appear to be flying?

Do you have the correct number of Quaffles and Bludgers?

Where would the stands be located in a Quidditch game, and how do you know?

Where are the referee (Madame Hooch) and the announcer (Lee Jordan) during the match?

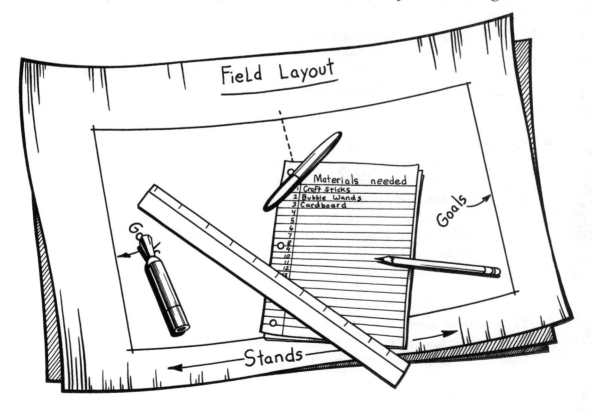

# Chapter Twelve: The Mirror of Erised
## Play a Game! – Creative Thinking

In Chapter Twelve, Ron teaches Harry how to play wizard chess. It is played "exactly like Muggle chess except that the figures [are] alive, which [makes] it a lot like directing troops in battle." Chess is a challenging game, which requires each opponent to think carefully before making a move. Knowing the rules is not enough; players must use strategy and logic to win the game.

**Create a new board game.**

Follow the directions below. Work with a group to create your own new game using information you have learned from *Harry Potter and the Sorcerer's Stone*. Put a check on the line next to each task as you complete it so that you will be organized and on track. Remember, since only Muggles will play your game, no real magic allowed!

1. **Brainstorm what kind of game you would like to create.**
   _____ What is the object of your game?
   _____ What does your game board look like?
   _____ What pieces will you use for the game?
   _____ What obstacles will you have in your game?
   _____ Will you have any characters (people or animals) in your game? If so, how will they move?
   _____ What other unique features will your game have?

2. **Create your game.**
   _____ Write the directions for your game.
   _____ Draw, color, or write any game cards you will need.
   _____ Collect objects (dice, spinner) you will need for the game.
   _____ Collect or create the game pieces that move around the board.

3. **Create your game board.**
   _____ Use a square piece of cardboard for the board (about 20" x 20").
   _____ Cover it with white drawing paper.
   _____ Using a pencil and a ruler, draw the layout of your game on the board.
   _____ Using a pencil, sketch in all the objects on your board.
   _____ With your group members, play the game to be sure you do not need to make any changes.
   _____ Finally, color your game board.

4. **Play your game!**
   Play your game with other groups, invite other classes to play with you, or store your game in the library for others to play.

# Chapter Twelve: The Mirror of Erised
## Your Deepest Desire – Writing Connection

In Chapter Twelve, Harry stumbles across the Mirror of Erised. When Harry looks in the mirror, he sees his family. Harry is mesmerized, and wants to sit and stare at the mirror for hours. However, when Ron gazes into the mirror, he sees himself as head boy. He is older, wearing a head boy badge and holding both the house cup and the Quidditch cup. Professor Dumbledore explains to Harry that the magical Mirror of Erised shows each person "the deepest, most desperate desire of our hearts."

**Describe your heart's desire.**

If you could look into the magical Mirror of Erised, what would you see? In the mirror below, draw a picture of what you most desire. In your journal, write a paragraph describing your drawing in detail. Explain why you would see this particular reflection.

## Find the Vocabulary

To help you find the words again, write the page number where you find each vocabulary word in the space next to it. Look up any words you don't know, and write their definitions in your journal.

| | | | | |
|---|---|---|---|---|
| ___ fanatic | ___ spluttered | ___ sinister | ___ mystified | ___ immortal |
| ___ biased | ___ shifty | ___ suspicious | ___ trowels | ___ furling |
| ___ spiral | ___ alibis | ___ meddle | ___ rebellion | ___ furor |
| ___ dappled | ___ imprecise | ___ sweltering | ___ omen | ___ skulking |
| ___ tottered | ___ threshold | ___ loathed | ___ spasm | ___ petrified |
| ___ vain | ___ agony | ___ hygienic | ___ sidled | ___ abysmal |

## Additional Activities

**Poetry:** Write a poem using as many vocabulary words as possible.

**Write a Song**: Using a familiar tune, make up a song about Harry Potter (you can use your poem from the exercise above if you can think of a tune that will go with the words). Use as many vocabulary words as possible.

**Be a Writer**: Write a short story using as many vocabulary words as you can. Be sure to use the words properly. See if you can relate your story to the book.

# Chapters Thirteen – Seventeen
## What Do You Know? – Comprehension

### Answer the following questions in your journal.

**Chapter Thirteen: Nicolas Flamel**

1. How does Harry acquire information about Nicholas Flamel? What does he find out about his age, whereabouts, and his accomplishments?

2. What are the powers of the Sorcerer's Stone?

3. What comparison does Draco Malfoy make between brains and gold concerning Neville? What is the true meaning of the statement?

4. Who is involved in a fight in the stands at the Quidditch game, and what is the fight about?

5. What does Harry do after the Quidditch game that could have been dangerous?

6. At the end of Chapter Thirteen, what information does Harry get about the Sorcerer's Stone? How does he get it and with whom does he share it?

**Chapter Fourteen: Norbert the Norwegian Ridgeback**

7. How do Harry, Ron, and Hermione treat Quirrell differently after Harry sees him talking to Snape in the forest?

8. What is Hagrid reading about in the library? Why?

9. How does Hermione get Hagrid to tell her about the guarding of the Sorcerer's Stone?

10. Who are the only two people who know how to get the Sorcerer's Stone?

11. Why does Ron write Charlie a letter? What is Charlie's response?

12. Who is Norbert and how is he transported out of Hogwarts?

13. Why are Harry and his friends so happy the night they are in the tower, and what happens to spoil their happiness?

**Chapter Fifteen: The Forbidden Forest**

14. How do other students treat Harry and his friends after they lose 150 house points?

15. Why is Harry in the forest and whom does he meet there?

16. What causes the sharp pain that Harry feels on his forehead while in the forest?

17. Who protects Harry from danger in the forest, and what does he explain about the planets and unicorn blood?

**Chapter Sixteen: Through the Trapdoor**

18. What keeps Harry up at night, and what does he think keeps causing his scar to hurt?

19. Why does Harry feel that he must go through the trapdoor that Fluffy is guarding?

20. What do Hermione and Ron do to show their true friendship for Harry?

21. What enchantments are used to protect the Sorcerer's Stone? Who cast them?

22. Describe how Harry and his friends get past each enchantment.

**Chapter Seventeen: The Man with Two Faces**

23. Who does Harry find in the last chamber? What does he tell Harry about the troll from Halloween, and Snape?

24. Why is the Mirror of Erised in the Chamber of Secrets, and how does Harry use it to get the Sorcerer's Stone?

25. Why does Harry consider the night of the final feast the best night of his life?

# Chapter Thirteen: Nicolas Flamel
## Back in Time – History Connection

In Chapter Thirteen, we learn that Nicolas Flamel has been alive for over six hundred years. In 1996, Nicolas Flamel celebrated his 665th birthday. Do the math in your journal. In what year was he born? _____

**Create a time line.**

Imagine all the events Flamel has lived through. Use the Internet and the library to research at least one major historical event for each century he was alive. You can use words and/or pictures to complete your time line. Use the time line below to take notes. Then, use drawing paper to complete your final product, or draw it in your journal. Compare your time line with others.

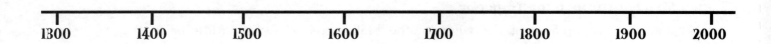

1300   1400   1500   1600   1700   1800   1900   2000

**Optional Activities:**

1.  Combine all of your time lines to create one large class time line with many different events in each century. Display your class time lines.

2.  Imagine you are Nicolas Flamel. Write a journal entry from his point of view about the most amazing change you have lived through in the past 665 years.

# Chapter Thirteen: Nicolas Flamel
## Be an Author! – Creative Writing

In Chapter Thirteen, we learn about Nicolas Flamel and his creation of the legendary Sorcerer's Stone. The Sorcerer's Stone has amazing magical abilities. It can turn any metal into gold and it can also make "the Elixir of Life, which will make the drinker immortal."

Consider this statement, and think about the word **legend**. A legend is a tale which may or may not be grounded in truth, and which is often passed from generation to generation. Examples of legendary characters and objects with which you may be familiar are Babe Ruth, King Arthur, the Loch Ness monster, and the fountain of youth.

### Write a legend.

In your journal, invent a legend of your own. You can use it to explain something from your own life, or make it up entirely. Ask yourself the following questions as you prepare to write:

**Is it an object, an animal, a person, or an event?**

**Does it explain a mysterious occurrence in nature (as does a myth)?**

**Is it based on a real-life experience, or is the entire story invented?**

After you have written your legend, allow two other students to read it. Can they determine if it is based on fact or entirely fictitious?

**Optional Activity:** Think about the powers of the Sorcerer's Stone and how having one would affect your life. If you were immortal, what would life be like? If you owned an object that would turn any metal into gold, how would your life be different? In your journal, list the pros and cons of owning the Sorcerer's Stone.

# Chapter Fourteen: Norbert the Norwegian Ridgeback
## Peculiar Pets – Science Connection

Hagrid wins a dragon egg from a stranger in the village in Chapter Fourteen. His research shows that the egg is that of a very rare, Norwegian Ridgeback dragon. When the egg hatches, Hagrid has a hard time caring for his pet, especially since it is illegal to own dragons and he can't let it be seen.

Hagrid loves pets, especially strange and unusual ones. He is sad when he says good-bye to his dragon that he named Norbert. Perhaps a new pet will cheer Hagrid up a bit. Pretend you are the owner of a pet shop on Diagon Alley. You specialize in strange and unusual pets. Harry, Hermione, and Ron are shopping for a new pet for Hagrid. Help them to choose a good pet.

**Create a "how-to" pamphlet about an unusual pet.**

1. Choose an unusual animal that you think Hagrid would enjoy owning.

2. Use an encyclopedia, the library, or the Internet to find information about your animal. Include the following information in your pamphlet:
   - The type of habitat this animal will need to survive
   - How and what to feed this animal as a baby and as an adult
   - General care information (food, sleeping habits, etc.)
   - How large it will become (height and weight)
   - Unusual behaviors the owner should know about

3. Create your pamphlet using a sheet of 11" x 17" paper folded into thirds. Make it colorful and attractive. Include the name of the pet and a large illustration of the animal on the cover.

# Chapter Fourteen: Norbert the Norwegian Ridgeback
## What An Adventure! – Creative Writing

In Chapter Fourteen, Harry and Hermione use Harry's invisibility cloak to bring Norbert, Hagrid's dragon, to the tallest tower at Hogwarts. Once there, some friends of Charlie Weasley take Norbert to Romania. What would you do with an invisibility cloak? Write a story about your adventure, using the story-writing process steps listed below (refer to page 19 for additional help).

The invisibility cloak comes in handy on many occasions. Harry's father once owned it, and now it belongs to Harry. When Harry receives it at Christmas, Ron tells Harry that invisibility cloaks are "really rare and *really* valuable." A note attached to the gift tells Harry to "use it well."

### Use the writing process for story writing.

**Prewriting** (Do this before writing your story.)
- Select a plot, characters, setting, time period in which the story takes place, etc.
- Do any necessary research for the story.
- Make an outline of your story.

**Writing Your First Draft** (Try not to edit at this stage.)
- Follow your outline to write your story, but if a better idea comes to you as you write, use it!
- Write as much detail as you can. Too much information is better than not enough, because you can always cut text when editing.
- If possible, put your story away for a few days before moving to the next writing stage.

**Revising** (You may want to have someone else read your story at this stage, before you revise.)
- Read your story over carefully to see if all your important ideas are included.
- Check to make sure you used your own words.
- Check to make sure your sentences are interesting, and that the story you have written is detailed and descriptive.

**Editing** (At this stage, check carefully for errors, and have a dictionary handy!)
- Check for spelling and punctuation errors.
- Trade papers with an editing partner.

**Preparing a Final Draft**
- Write your final draft of your story in your best handwriting, or type it on a computer.

# Chapter Fourteen: Norbert the Norwegian Ridgeback
## Dragons In Romania! – Geography Connection

In Chapter Fourteen, Harry, Ron, and Hermione help Hagrid relocate his dragon to Romania. Ron's brother, Charlie, lives there while studying dragons. Where is Romania located? What other information can you find out about it?

**Find out about Romania.**

Look at the map of Eastern Europe below. Use your social studies book, an atlas, an encyclopedia, or the Internet to locate Romania. **Draw** a dragon over the area where you would find it. **Label** the continents and the major oceans of the world. **Fill in** the fact sheet for Romania.

**Romania Fact Sheet**

1. Continent: _____

2. Location on that continent: _____

3. Population: _____

4. Size: _____

5. Capital: _____

6. Bordering Countries: _____

7. Other Interesting Facts: _____

   _____

   _____

**Optional Activity**: Research dragons. Are they real or fictitious? Write a short report about them.

# Chapter Fifteen: The Forbidden Forest
## What's Lurking in the Dark? – Science Connection

In Chapter Fifteen, Harry, Hermione, Neville, and Malfoy receive notes telling them that their detention will take place at eleven o'clock that same night. They are very frightened to learn that their detention includes going into the forest, which is off-limits to them normally. They soon learn that they are trying to locate a wounded unicorn. Hagrid tells them to follow the "silvery stuff" (unicorn blood), but to stay on the path. What's lurking in the dark? What has harmed the unicorn?

**Write a report.**

Although the forest houses many creatures that we would not find in a normal forest, there are still many interesting animals that make their homes in real forests. Research a forest community (it may be located anywhere in the world). Use the library, the Internet, a science textbook, or an encyclopedia for your research. Choose an interesting animal from the forest community. Research the animal, and write a report to share your findings. Use the guide below to plan your report.

**Paragraph 1 (Introduction)**
- Location of the forest in which your animal lives (include continent and country, as well as region within the country)
- Characteristics of that forest (types of trees, plants, and other animals that live there)

**Paragraph 2**
- Name of animal (include genus and species)
- Physical features (appearance, height, weight)

**Paragraph 3**
- Food and hunting (What do they eat? How do they get it?)
- What hunts this animal? What are its predators?

**Paragraph 4**
- Breeding (mating season, number of young)
- Lifespan (How long do they usually live?)

**Paragraph 5**
- Habits (What is the behavior of this animal? How does this animal spend its time? Does it roam? Is it a solitary creature? When is it active?)

**Paragraph 6**
- Interesting or unusual facts about the animal

**Paragraph 7 (Summary/Conclusion)**
- Status of the animal. Is it endangered, threatened, or is the survival rate of the species healthy?

# Chapter Fifteen: The Forbidden Forest
## Legendary Beasts – Mythology Connection

There are amazing creatures lurking in the Forbidden Forest, such as unicorns and centaurs. Although the unicorn seen by Harry and his friends has unfortunately been killed, several centaurs have conversations with Hagrid and the students.

### Research mythical beasts.

1. Do some research on centaurs and unicorns. Where did tales of these mythical beasts originate? What else can you find out about centaurs and unicorns?

2. Compare your research to the way J. K. Rowling describes the beasts in *Harry Potter and the Sorcerer's Stone*. How does the research differ from what is said in the book about unicorns and centaurs? How is it similar? Record the similarities and differences on the lines below.

**Unicorns in *Harry Potter and the Sorcerer's Stone***

_____
_____
_____
_____
_____
_____

**Research about Unicorns in Myths and Legends**

_____
_____
_____
_____
_____
_____

**Centaurs in *Harry Potter and the Sorcerer's Stone***

_____
_____
_____
_____
_____
_____

**Research about Centaurs in Myths and Legends**

_____
_____
_____
_____
_____
_____

**Optional Activity**: If there are differences between the characters of legends and their treatment in the novel, why do you think the author made that decision? Write your thoughts in your journal.

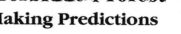  

# Chapter Fifteen: The Forbidden Forest
## What's Their Secret? – Making Predictions

In Chapter Fifteen, Harry, Ron and Hermione are convinced that Professor Snape is trying to steal the Sorcerer's Stone, and that Professor Quirrell has given in and told Snape how to get past his Anti-Dark Force Spell. If Dumbledore has had each professor at Hogwarts use a spell to protect the Sorcerer's Stone, then Snape would only know how to get past two of them — Quirrell's and his own.

Knowing what you do about each professor and what subject they teach, predict what kind of spell each one might have cast to protect the stone. Example: Hagrid, Keeper of Keys and Grounds at Hogwarts, loves monstrous animals. Therefore, it is logical that he is the one who loaned Dumbledore his three-headed dog, Fluffy, to guard the stone.

**Fill in the chart below. Think like the teachers might, then make your predictions. To help you along, here is a list of the professors and the classes they teach.**

| Professor | Class Professor Teaches | Spell Professor Might Have Cast |
|---|---|---|
| Professor Sprout | Herbology | |
| Professor Binns | History of Magic | |
| Professor Flitwick | Charms | |
| Professor Quirrell | Defense Against the Dark Arts | |
| Professor McGonagall | Transfiguration | |
| Professor Snape | Potions | |
| Professor Dumbledore | Headmaster at Hogwarts | |

# Chapter Sixteen: Through the Trapdoor
## Magical Mush – Science Connection

During exams, Harry and the other students were asked to conjure up potions and cast spells. Try your own hand at creating a mixture that appears to have magical powers.

**Make (but don't eat!) this "Magical Mush."**

**Materials (for each group of 4-6)**
1 box of cornstarch (1 lb.)
1²/₃ cups of water
5 drops of blue or green food coloring (optional)
Newspaper
Mixing bowl

**Procedure**
1. Before you begin, cover the entire work area with newspaper.
2. Pour about half of the water into a mixing bowl.
3. Add food coloring to the water, if desired.
4. Add the cornstarch.
5. Add the remaining water.
6. Combine the ingredients by lifting the mixture from bottom to top (folding it together) until blended.

**Activities: Record what happens after each step. Write your findings in your journal.**
1. Slowly dip your finger into the magical mush. Slowly remove your finger.
2. With a fist, punch the mush lightly, but quickly.
3. Try placing some mush on the desk.
4. Try rolling the mush into a ball with your hands.
5. Try floating several objects on the mush.
6. Try to stir the mush quickly with a spoon.
7. Think of any other experiments to try with your mush.
8. After experimenting with the magical mush, brainstorm with your group why this mixture behaves the way it does. What happens to make this mush appear magical? Discuss your ideas.

**Optional Activity**: In your groups, brainstorm uses for this mush. Can you find a way to use this mush that you can sell to the public? What would you use it to do? What would you name it? How would you market it? Who would buy it? How much would you charge for it? Create a poster advertising your new product.

# Chapter Sixteen: Through the Trapdoor
## The Puzzler – Math Connection

Harry and Hermione face a complicated logic puzzle in one of the chambers. Hermione notes that, "A lot of the greatest wizards haven't got an ounce of logic, they'd be stuck in here forever." Indeed, they cannot use magic to solve the puzzle, only reasoning.

### Solve the problem.

Work alone or with a partner to try to solve the following logic problem. As with all word problems, draw pictures, make charts, etc. Be patient and keep trying!

**Harry needs to purchase several books for his first term at Hogwarts. Based upon the information given, rank all of the books from the most costly to the least expensive.**

1. *The Standard Book of Spells* is more expensive than *One Thousand Magical Herbs and Fungi*, but less expensive then *A Beginners' Guide to Transfiguration*, which cost 35 Galleons.

2. *Fantastic Beasts and Where to Find Them* costs 50 Galleons and is twice as much as *Standard Book of Spells*.

3. *The Dark Forces: A Guide to Self-Protection* costs 5 more Galleons than *Fantastic Beasts and Where to Find Them*.

4. *Magical Drafts and Potions* costs more than *One Thousand Magical Herbs and Fungi*.

5. *Magical Theory* is $\frac{1}{2}$ the price of *Magical Drafts and Potions*.

6. *A History of Magic* costs 8 Galleons less than *Magical Theory* and 15 Galleons less than *The Standard Book of Spells*.

7. *A Beginners' Guide to Transfiguration* costs one Galleon less than *Magical Drafts and Potions*.

8. *One Thousand Magical Herbs and Fungi* costs one Galleon more than *Magical Theory*.

# Chapter Seventeen: The Man with Two Faces
## What Is the Truth? – Making Predictions

*Harry Potter and the Sorcerer's Stone* is only the first book in a series of seven books. After Harry's encounter with Voldemort, he asks Professor Dumbledore why Voldemort wanted him destroyed. Dumbledore mysteriously tells him. "Alas, the first thing you ask me, I cannot tell you...when you are ready, you will know."

What do you think Dumbledore means by this? What reasons would he have to keep Harry from knowing about his future in regards to Voldemort? Think about how the series might proceed, and make some predictions about the futures of some of the characters. Ask yourself questions like: Does Harry defeat Voldemort in the end? What does Harry do when he grows up? Does Hermione graduate at the top of her class? Will Ron ever be head boy? What happens to Neville? To Malfoy? Will Professor Snape ever teach Defense Against the Dark Arts?

### Make predictions.
Next to each character listed below, write a prediction for his or her future. Compare your predictions with the actual text, and see how much "evidence" you can find to back up your guesses. Then, compare your list to other students' lists. Who agrees with your guesses?

**Harry Potter** _____

**Ron Weasley** _____

**Hermione Granger** _____

**Albus Dumbledore** _____

**Professor Snape** _____

**Draco Malfoy** _____

**Rubeus Hagrid** _____

**Neville Longbottom** _____

_____

**Voldemort** _____

_____

# Final Assessment
## What do you know? – Open-Ended Questions

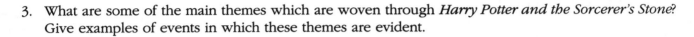

## Answer the following questions in your journal.

1. Who is Harry Potter and why is he special?

2. Why is he brought to the Dursley family?

3. What are some of the main themes which are woven through *Harry Potter and the Sorcerer's Stone?* Give examples of events in which these themes are evident.

4. At the Dursley home, Harry sleeps in a cupboard under the staircase. How do you think he feels about this? How would you feel?

5. How do you think Harry's life would have been different if his parents were still alive?

6. Why do you think Harry survived the night his parents died?

7. How do you think Dudley feels once he finds out Harry is a wizard? Does Dudley's attitude toward Harry change? If so, how?

8. Why does Harry believe that ordinary people could not see the Leaky Cauldron?

9. When Harry is worried about being famous and living up to everyone's expectations, what advice does Hagrid give him?

10. What are the good points about each house at Hogwarts? Using this information, could there also be any bad points about each house? If so, what are they?

11. What do you think a treacle tart is? What about a rock cake? A stoat sandwich? Are there any other foods mentioned that were unfamiliar? What are they?

12. What does Harry dream about on his first night at Hogwarts? What do you think the dream means?

13. Who does Harry dislike most, Dudley Dursley or Draco Malfoy? Why?

14. Of all the characters, which one would you be most likely to choose as a friend, and why?

15. Harry is extremely nervous before his first Quidditch game. Does his nervousness help him or hinder his performance?

16. Hermione tells a lie to keep Ron and Harry from getting in trouble when they trapped the mountain troll. Did she do the right thing? Could she have gotten them out of trouble without lying? If so, how?

17. Do the seasons change at Hogwarts? List clues from the text that tell you the answer.

18. Why doesn't Harry go home for Christmas?

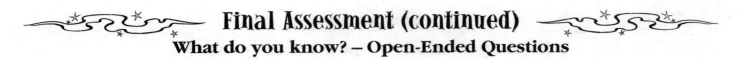

19. Harry receives several nice things for Christmas. If you could send Harry a present, what would it be?

20. What is the meaning of this statement that Dumbledore makes to Harry, regarding the Mirror of Erised: "It does not do to dwell on dreams and forget to live..."

21. Why do you think that Harry and Hermione forget the invisibility cloak and leave it in the tower on the night they get rid of Norbert?

22. How do you think Harry and his friends feel about losing 150 points for Gryffindor? Find quotes in the text that support your answer.

23. Do you think Harry, Ron, Neville, and Hermione are treated fairly by the other students after they lost points? Why or why not?

24. When Ronan tells Harry, "The forest holds many secrets," what do you think he means?

25. What do you think the planets are predicting that causes Firenze to hope they are being read incorrectly?

26. When Dumbledore says, "Humans have a knack of choosing precisely those things that are worst for them," what does he mean?

27. What do you think might have happened if the Sorcerer's Stone had not been destroyed?

# Optional Final Journal Entry Topics
## Choose one or more of these topics to write about in your journal.

1. If you could invent another Hogwarts house, what would its qualities be? Which animal would be its mascot and why?

2. Look back at question #16. Do you think it is ever right to lie? Why or why not?

3. Reread question #15. Describe a time when you were very nervous about performing a task. How well did you do the task? Would you be nervous about doing this task again?

4. Use the description in the book to draw a picture of Norbert.

5. Refer to question #23. Can you think of a time when you disappointed a friend? What happened and how did you feel?

**\* Please note**: Many questions in this book are open-ended and require students to interpret the novel. Therefore, you should expect to get many different answers from your students. In places where the answer key lists *Answers will vary*, use your best judgment as to what makes a reasonable answer. Some guidelines have been provided for you, especially where the answers come from the text.

**\* Also note**: The vocabulary definitions were created with special attention to the context which they were written. Some of the definitions are British, and others are different from the usual dictionary definitions.

**Page 10:**

**tawny**—a light brown to brownish-orange color
**tantrum**—a fit of bad temper
**chortled**—to combine a chuckle and a snort
**peculiar**—unusual; strange
**enraged**—angered; made furious
**pursed**—puckered
**quiver**—tremble
**rummaging**—looking for something
**faltered**—hesitated
**cupboard**—a small closet used for storage
**frantically**—excitedly with strong emotion or frustration
**hoodlums**—unruly, rough thugs or young people
**specimen**—an animal meant to be representative of its species
**deafening**—very loud
**gibber**—talk nonsense
**knickerbockers**—short pants gathered at the knee
**knobbly**—covered in small bumps

**parchment**—writing paper made to look like the skin of a sheep or goat which has been prepared for writing (the skin is also called parchment)
**wheezed**—spoke with a hoarse whistling sound
**trodden**—crushed beneath the feet; trampled
**tufts**—clumps of hair
**bewildered**—confused; dazed
**quailed**—shrunk in fear
**headmaster**—the principal of a school
**rubbish**—nonsense
**gargoyles**—a monstrous figure
**trances**—spells; hypnotic states
**ruefully**—regretfully
**gamekeeper**—a person who hunts and/or protects wildlife
**dormice**—small European rodents

**Page 11:**

**Chapter One: The Boy Who Lived**
**1.** Harry's aunt and uncle live at #4 Privet Drive, Little Whinging, Surrey, England.
**2.** He notices a cat reading a map, strangely-dressed people, hearing the word Muggle, and whispers about the Potters. The news broadcast says that owls are flying all over the country and there are a lot of shooting stars.
**3.** Professor McGonagall
**4.** Dumbledore arrives to oversee the plan for bringing Harry to his aunt and uncle.
**5.** Hagrid arrives by flying motorcycle, which he has borrowed from Sirius Black.
**6.** Dumbledore, McGonagall, and Hagrid discuss details about the downfall of Voldemort and the death of James and Lily Potter.

**Chapter Two: The Vanishing Glass**
**7.** Other events are: the time Harry's hair grew back overnight, the time he made an old sweater of Dudley's shrink to nothing, and the time he landed on the chimney of the school.
**8.** The glass wall of a boa constrictor cage disappears, allowing the snake to escape. Harry appears to be talking to the snake when it happens.
**9.** Mr. Dursley gets mad about Harry's dream of riding a flying motorcycle. Harry sees a blinding flash of green light when he tries to remember the car crash.

**Chapter Two: The Vanishing Glass (continued)**
**10.** A tiny man in a violet top hat bows to him in the street. An old, wild-looking woman in green waves to him on a bus. A bald man in purple coat shakes his hand on the street.
**11.** The people seem to vanish when Harry tries to take a closer look.
**12.** Everyone at the school is afraid of Dudley and his friends, so they avoid Harry.

**Chapter Three: The Letters from No One**
**13.** The letter is addressed to Mr. H. Potter, The Cupboard under the Stairs, #4 Privet Drive, Little Whinging, Surrey. Mr. Dursley grabs the letter from Harry and burns it.
**14.** They appear upset, nervous, frightened and angry.
**15.** Mr. Dursley realizes someone knows Harry lives in the cupboard.
**16.** First, Mr. Dursley nails up the mail slot, then he drives the family to a hotel, then he takes them to hide in a hut on a rock that is out in the sea.
**17.** The address changes.

**Chapter Four: The Keeper of the Keys**
**18.** Someone knocks on the door, the door swings off its hinges, and Hagrid arrives.

**Page 11 (continued):**

**Chapter Four: The Keeper of the Keys (continued)**

**19.** Hagrid is the size of a giant. He ties a rifle in knots, conjures a fire, carries odd things in his pockets, has been arranging for the letters to follow Harry, and sends a letter by owl post. His umbrella's flash of violet light causes a curly pig's tail to appear on Dudley. Hagrid also says he's not supposed to do magic (implying that he is capable).

**20.** "Muggles" is the wizard term for non-magical people.

**21.** When Harry was one year old, Voldemort tried to kill him with a curse. Instead, Harry survived with a scar on his forehead. Voldemort lost all of his powers and disappeared.

**Chapter Four: The Keeper of the Keys (continued)**

**22.** Hagrid uses the owl to send a letter to Dumbledore.

**23.** Voldemort is a Dark Wizard (a wizard who uses his powers to harm people). He led a band of Dark Wizards who did evil deeds, including killing wizards and Muggles.

**24.** Professor McGonagall has sent the letter to inform Harry that he has been accepted to Hogwarts, a witchcraft and wizarding school.

**25.** Hagrid asks "Never made things happen when you was scared or angry?" See #7 – #8 for more information.

**Page 12:** The first time line may include the following: waking up, leaving for work at 8:30, seeing a cat reading a map, driving to work, seeing odd people, arriving at work, yelling at people, making telephone calls, having lunch, hearing Harry Potter's name, dialing his phone number, running into a strange man, arriving at home, seeing the cat again, having dinner, talking to his wife, watching the news, mentioning the strange events happening, getting into bed, and going to sleep.

**Page 13:** Answers will vary.

**Page 14:**

| | Cause | Effect |
|---|---|---|
| 1. | **There are many spiders in Harry's cupboard.** | Harry is used to spiders. |
| 2. | The only clothes Harry owns are Dudley's old clothes that are about four sizes too big for him. | **Harry looks smaller and skinnier than he is.** |
| 3. | **Dudley has only thirty-six presents.** | Dudley is on the verge of a tantrum. |
| 4. | Mrs. Figgs phones to say she has broken her leg and cannot watch Harry. | **Harry goes to the zoo.** |
| 5. | **Aunt Petunia dislikes Harry's hair.** | Aunt Petunia cuts Harry's hair very short, leaving only bangs to hide his scar. |
| 6. | **Dudley's gang chases Harry.** | Harry ends up sitting on the chimney. |
| 7. | Harry thinks the boa constrictor must be bored living in one tank all its life. | **The snake opens its eyes, raises its head, and winks.** |
| 8. | Uncle Vernon is very angry after the snake incident. | **Harry is sent to his cupboard without meals.** |
| 9. | **Dudley's gang hates Harry. No one likes to disagree with them.** | Harry has no friends in school. |

**Page 15:** Descriptions may include: **1.** Harry sleeps in a cupboard full of spiders. **2.** He is Dudley's punching bag. **3.** He wears Dudley's old clothes. **3.** He isn't allowed to ask about his parents. **4.** His uncle speaks unkindly to him. **5.** His aunt, uncle, and cousin don't want him to go the zoo. **6.** The Dursleys speak of Harry as if he isn't there or as if he is disgusting. **7.** The Dursleys don't want to buy Harry ice cream. **8.** Uncle Vernon likes to complain about Harry. **9.** Harry is sent to bed without meals.

**Page 16:** Answers will vary.

**Page 17:** Sample answers are listed below.

### Beginning of the Chapter

**1.**

| Character | Attitude toward Harry | Example to support your statement |
|---|---|---|
| Uncle Vernon | no respect for Harry | makes him live in cupboard |
| Aunt Petunia | resentful of Harry | speaks harshly to Harry |
| Dudley | superior and cruel | chases and teases Harry constantly |

### Middle of the Chapter

**2.**

| Character | Attitude toward Harry | Example to support your statement |
|---|---|---|
| Uncle Vernon | nervous | moves Harry to bedroom |
| Aunt Petunia | nervous | afraid someone is watching the house |
| Dudley | shocked and amazed | hits his mother, is sick on purpose, tries to get his room back |

### End of the Chapter

**3.**

| Character | Attitude toward Harry | Example to support your statement |
|---|---|---|
| Uncle Vernon | frightened | hides with his family in a broken-down hut |
| Aunt Petunia | frightened | suggests they go home |
| Dudley | resentful | complains when he misses his favorite TV show |

**Page 18:** 1. "...you could make out his eyes, glinting like black beetles under all the hair." 2. "...Uncle Vernon made another funny noise, like a mouse being trodden on." 3. "Harry felt the warmth wash over him as though he'd sunk into a hot bath." 4. "Questions exploded inside Harry's head like fireworks..." 5. "Then he came back and sat down as though this was as normal as talking on the telephone." 6. "Hagrid suddenly pulled out a very dirty, spotted handkerchief and blew his nose with a sound like a foghorn." 7. "Pointing this at Uncle Vernon like a sword..." 8. "If he'd once defeated the greatest sorcerer in the world, how come Dudley had always been able to kick him around like a football?" 9. "He brought the umbrella swishing down through the air to point at Dudley – there was a flash of violet light, a sound like a firecracker..." 10. "...he was so much like a pig anyway there wasn't much left ter do."

**Page 19:** Summaries should include the deadly encounter between Harry's wizard parents and Voldemort and Harry's arrival at the Dursleys' home.

**Page 20:**

**collapsed**—something that has broken or fallen apart
**savaging**—attacking viciously
**enchantment**—a magical spell
**vaults**—safe chambers for protecting items of value
**clambered**—climbed
**transfiguration**—the art of changing of one thing into another
**cauldron**—a very large pot for boiling
**bloke**—British slang for man
**hag**—a witch or sorceress
**Apothecary**—a place where medicines are sold
**prickled**—tingled
**gawking**—staring; gaping
**ruddy**—having a reddish color
**jostled**—pushed or shoved
**corridor**—hallway

**astonishment**—amazement
**wailed**—cried out
**stunned**—surprised
**dumbfounded**—baffled; confused
**riffraff**—disreputable people
**drone**—a steady low humming sound
**chamber**—a room or hall
**dormitory**—living quarters for students
**toil**—hard work
**sallow**—pale, sickly color
**poltergeist**—a mischievous ghost
**subtle**—difficult to understand or distinguish
**ensnaring**—capturing
**bewitching**—casting a spell on
**crossbow**—a short bow mounted crosswise near the end of a wooden stock that shoots short arrows

**Page 21:**
### Chapter Five: Diagon Alley
**1.** Hagrid flies to the hut, leaves by boat, and uses his umbrella to make the boat speed to land.
**2.** Gringotts is a wizard bank hundreds of miles under London. It is run by goblins. Most Muggles don't know it exists. Goblins are scary and use powerful magic to keep wizard money safe.
**3.** Cornelius Fudge. His job is to keep the secret from Muggles that witches and wizards still exist.
**4.** The brother wand (made with a feather from the same phoenix) gave Harry his scar.
**5.** The brother wand belonged to Voldemort who did great, yet terrible, things.
**6.** Harry reports to Hogwarts September 1, He takes the train from King's Cross, at platform nine and three-quarters.
### Chapter Six: The Journey from Platform Nine and Three-Quarters
**7.** Harry sees others going through the wall between platforms nine and ten. Mrs. Weasley tells him how to get through.
**8.** He meets the Weasleys, Hermione Granger, Draco Malfoy, Crabbe, Goyle, Neville Longbottom. People recognize his scar and name.
**9.** "Loads of Owls" means lots of letters.
**10.** Albus Dumbledore, Morgana, Hengist of Woodcroft, Alberic Grunnion, Circe, Paracelsus, Merlin, Cliodna.
**11.** Dumbledore is the greatest wizard of modern times. He defeated the dark wizard Grindelwald in 1945, discovered twelve uses of dragon's blood, and worked on alchemy with Nicholas Flamel.
**12.** Aunt Petunia vacuums, they watch television, students are wearing sneakers and jeans, etc. Answers will vary.
**13.** Draco's Malfoy family was one of the first to come back to good side after Voldemort disappeared. They said they'd been bewitched. Ron's father did not believe them.
### Chapter Seven: The Sorting Hat
**14.** The sorting hat is a special hat that talks, reads minds, and decides in which house to place first year students.

### Chapter Seven: The Sorting Hat (continued)
**15.** Gryffindors are brave at heart, daring, have nerve and are chivalrous. Hufflepuffs are just, loyal, patient, true, and unafraid of toil. Ravenclaws are wise, ready-minded, quick-witted. Slytherins are real friends, cunning, and use any means to achieve their ends.
**16.** Magical things include: talking ghosts, candles floating over the tables, bewitched ceiling, singing hat, food appears on tables, plates clean themselves, pain in Harry's scar, reminder not to use magic in corridors, magic wand, golden ribbon of words, floating walking sticks, portrait in wall talks and opens.
**17.** Dumbledore says "Nitwit! Blubber! Oddment! Tweak!" Food appears, including roast beef, chicken, pork chops, lamb chops, sausages, bacon, steak, potatoes (boiled, roasted, and fried), Yorkshire pudding, peas, carrots, gravy, ketchup, peppermint humbugs, ice cream, apple pie, treacle treats, chocolate éclairs, jam doughnuts, trifle, strawberries, Jell-O®, rice pudding.
**18.** The forest, because it is full of dangerous beasts, and the third floor corridor on the right side of the castle (no reason given).
### Chapter Eight: The Potions Master
**19.** There are 142 staircases. They are wide, sweeping, rickety, some lead somewhere different on Fridays, some have vanishing steps.
**20.** Portraits speak, move around, and leave the frames. Some doors have to be tickled or asked to open, some are really just solid walls that look like doors.
**21.** Peeves tricks students so they do not get to class on time.
**22.** "...to bottle fame, brew glory, even stopper death." Answers about the meanings of these will vary.
**23.** Harry didn't warn Neville not to add quills to his potion and he was sarcastic to Snape.
**24.** Harry thinks Snape hates him because of the treatment, ridicule, and loss of points Harry suffers from Snape.
**25.** He and Hagrid were at Gringott's on the day it was robbed.

**Page 22:** Harry buys 8 books, 6 pieces of clothing (a pair of gloves counts as one piece), 5 pieces of equipment, and 1 animal, for a total of 20 items. So, 40% of his purchase is books, 30% clothing, 25% equipment, and 5% animals. Pie graphs will differ in appearance, but should be divided and labeled similarly to the one at right.

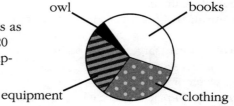

**Page 23:** **1.** 119 Sickles **2.** 4,437 Knuts, 153 Sickles, 9 Galleons **3.** 493 Knuts. **4.** 51 Sickles, 3 Galleons. **5.** 187 Sickles, 11 Galleons **6.** 2 Galleons **7.** The Dark Forces – 10 Galleons, Magical Drafts and Potions – 6 Galleons, Fantastic Beasts and Where To Find Them – 5 Galleons **8.** 50 Galleons, 850 Sickles, 24,650 Knuts

**Page 24:**
**1. - 2. See labeled map, right**
**3. Area** – 94,251 square miles
**Population** – 57,730,000 (2000 census)
**Capital** – London
**Largest City** – London
**Highest Point** – In England = Scafell Pike, 3,210 ft. above sea level. In Scotland = Ben Nevis, 4,406 ft. above sea level
**4. Answers will vary**

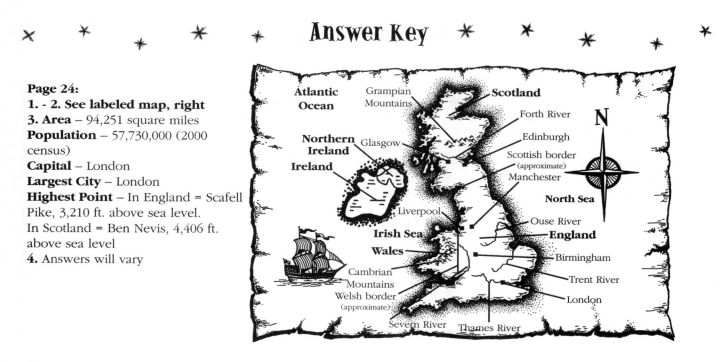

**Page 25:** Answers may include: dark, thick trees, narrow path, great, black lake, starry sky, vast castle, smooth as glass (lake), curtain of ivy, dark tunnel, smooth, damp grass.

**Page 26:** **1. Professor McGonagall:** tall, black hair, wearing emerald green robes, stern face, is not someone to cross **2. Professor Dumbledore:** sits in the center of the teachers' table, silver hair shines as brightly as the ghosts, beams at students as if happy to see them **3. Professor Quirrell:** wears a turban. From Chapter Five: pale, young, nervous, stammers **4. Professor Snape:** greasy black hair, hooked nose, sallow skin. When he looks at Harry, Harry feels pain in his scar

**Page 27:** **1. Gryffindor:** brave at heart, daring, nerve, chivalry **2. Hufflepuff:** just, loyal, patient, true, unafraid of toil **3. Ravenclaw:** wise, old ready mind, wit, learning **4. Slytherin:** real friends, cunning, use any means to achieve their ends

| Gryffindor | Hufflepuff | Ravenclaw | Slytherin |
|---|---|---|---|
| Lavender Brown | Fat Friar [ghost] | Terry Boot | Millicent Bulstrode |
| Seamus Finnigan | Hannah Abbott | Mandy Brocklehurst | Draco Malfoy |
| Hermione Granger | Susan Bones | Lisa Turpin | Crabbe |
| Neville Longbottom | Justin Finch-Fletchley | | Goyle |
| Harry Potter | **Add Later:** | | Blaise Zabini |
| Dean Thomas | Professor Sprout | | Bloody Baron [ghost] |
| Ron Weasley | | | Professor Snape |
| Percy Weasley | | | **Add Later:** |
| Fred Weasley | | | Marcus Flint |
| George Weasley | | | Adrian Pucey |
| Nearly Headless Nick [ghost] | | | Terence Higgs |
| Professor McGonagall | | | Bletchley |
| **Add Later:** | | | Pansy Parkinson |
| Angelina Johnson | | | |
| Oliver Wood | | | |
| Alicia Spinnet | | | |
| Katie Bell | | | |
| Lee Jordan | | | |
| Parvati Patil | | | |

**Page 28:** (Note: ghosts are considered people for this exercise.)

| People | | Places | Things | |
|---|---|---|---|---|
| Harry Potter | Hermione Granger | Hogwarts | Friday | Potions |
| Nearly Headless Nick | Seamus Finnigan | Romania | Mrs. Norris | Hedwig |
| Gryffindors | Muggle | Great Hall | Wednesday | One Thousand |
| Peeves the Poltergeist | Slytherins | Slytherin House | Herbology | Magical Herbs and |
| Argus Filch | Professor Snape | Gryffindor House | History of Magic | Fungi |
| Ron | Hagrid | Gringotts | Charms | Draught of Living |
| Professor Quirrell | Draco Malfoy | | Transfiguration | Death |
| Weasley twins | Crabbe | | Defense Against the | Fang |
| Professor Sprout | Goyle | | Dark Arts | *Daily Prophet* |
| Professor Binns | the Dursleys' | | Double Potions | July |
| Emeric the Evil | Neville | | | |
| Uric the Oddball | Fred | | | |
| Professor Flitwick | George | | | |
| Professor McGonagall | Charlie | | | |

**Page 29:** Professor Snape – Potions; Professor Binns – History of Magic; Professor Flitwick – Charms; Professor McGonagall – Transfiguration; Professor Sprout – Herbology; Quirrell – Defense Against the Dark Arts
**1.** History of Magic **2.** Professor Sprout **3.** Potions **4.** Charms **5.** Professor Snape **6.** Transfiguration

**Page 30:**

**boastful**—to speak highly of oneself
**extraordinary**—highly unusual
**quaver**—tremble
**javelin**—a spear
**triumphant**—joyful and proud for a successful achievement of some sort
**looming**—appearing in view
**embers**—hot coals from a fire
**hurtled**—traveled rapidly
**bellowed**—yelled; shouted
**snarled**—spoke threateningly
**impatient**—unwilling to wait
**griffin**—an imaginary creature with the head and wings of an eagle and the body of a lion
**waggled**—shook back and forth
**slouched**—walked in a clumsy, lazy manner
**echoes**—repeated sounds that bounce off of walls or objects
**berserk**—crazy
**flailed**—swung wildly

**championship**—competition or contest to determine a winner
**conjured**—brought about through magical or mysterious means
**mangled**—injured badly
**diversion**—a distraction
**jinxing**—causing bad things to happen to someone or something
**brandished**—pointed something at someone in a threatening manner
**askew**—off center
**chipolatas**—small pork sausages
**crackers**—party favors (containing small gifts) that make a loud sound when pulled apart
**crumpets**—a small, flat, round piece of bread, baked on a griddle and usually served toasted
**eerie**—causing fear, dread, or uneasiness; strange and frightening
**earsplitting**—loud enough to hurt the ears
**inscription**—words carved into a solid object

**Page 31:**

**Chapter Nine: The Midnight Duel**
**1.** A Remembrall tells its owner that he or she has forgotten to do something. Neville receives one from his grandmother.
**2.** He disobeys Madame Hooch and flies on his broom. When Professor McGonagall sees how good he is, she places him on the Gryffindor Quidditch team as the Seeker.

**Chapter Nine: The Midnight Duel (continued)**
**3.** Duel with wand only, no contact, a second wizard takes over if you die. He would lose points for Gryffindor.
**4.** When Harry and his friends arrive in the trophy room, they hear noises in the next room, they know Filch and Mrs. Norris are there, then they meet Peeves and have to run away in order to avoid getting caught.

**Chapter Nine: The Midnight Duel (continued)**
**5.** He is in the forbidden right-hand corridor on the third floor, looking into the eyes of a monstrous dog.
**6.** Three heads, three pairs of rolling mad eyes, three noses quivering and twitching, three drooling mouths, saliva hanging in slippery ropes from yellowish fangs. Harry thinks it is protecting the package from Gringotts.
**Chapter Ten: Halloween**
**7.** A Nimbus Two Thousand broomstick.
**8.** Quidditch is a game played in the air by two teams of seven players each. The Keeper protects the goals and keeps the opposing team from scoring. The Beaters hit Bludgers (flying black balls that try to hit all of the players) towards opponents. The Chasers try to send the Quaffles (red flying balls) though the goals. The Seeker tries to catch the Golden Snitch, which is worth 150 points and usually ends the game.
**9.** Harry has never played before, and Seekers usually have the worst accidents while playing.
**10.** A troll was loose in the castle.
**11.** Harry and Ron defeat the troll. Harry sticks his wand tip in its nose, and Ron knocks it out with his own club.
**12.** Hermione lied and said that she was trying to defeat it, and they all could have been killed. She keeps them out of trouble so they are her friends.
**Chapter Eleven: Quidditch**
**13.** In Quidditch, there are 700 ways of committing a foul, all of which happened in World Cup of 1473. Seekers are usually the smallest, fastest players, and most serious accidents happen to Seekers. No one has ever died playing Quidditch, although several referees have vanished and turn up in the Sahara Desert.
**14.** Harry thinks he was bitten by Fluffy. Hermione disagrees because she doesn't think Snape would steal from Dumbledore.

**Chapter Eleven: Quidditch (continued)**
**15.** Dean is comparing the foul to getting a red card in soccer.
**16.** Fluffy is a monstrous, three-headed dog, which Hagrid bought from a Greek he met in the pub.
**17.** Professor Flitwick covers the tree branches with golden bubbles from his wand.
**18.** Hagrid claims that Snape wouldn't try to harm Harry or another student.
**Chapter Twelve: The Mirror of Erised**
**19.** The Weasley children stay at Hogwarts for Christmas because Mr. and Mrs. Weasley are going to Romania to visit their son Charlie.
**20.** Harry receives six presents: a wooden flute from Hagrid; a fifty-pence piece from the Dursleys; a sweater and homemade fudge from Mrs. Weasley; Chocolate Frogs from Hermione; and an invisibility cloak that used to belong to his father, from an anonymous giver.
**21.** The special gift is an invisibility cloak. Answers will vary.
**22.** Crackers are party favors filled with gifts, which make a noise when they are pulled apart. Wizard crackers have magical prizes. Harry gets several white mice; a rear admiral's hat; a pack of non-explodable, luminous balloons; a Grow-Your-Own-Warts kit; and a new wizard chess set.
**23.** Harry goes to the restricted section of the library, then he goes to a room with the Mirror of Erised.
**24.** It shows anyone who stands in front of it their deepest desire. Harry sees his family, because he has never known them. Ron sees himself as head boy and the Quidditch captain, because he has always been outshadowed by his brothers. Student drawings will vary.
**25.** Dumbledore advises Harry not to look for the mirror again, saying, "It does not do to dwell on dreams and forget to live."

**Page 32:** Poems will vary.

**Page 33:** **1. was there in a flash** = immediately or quickly **2. Neville was hanging on to her every word** = listening very intently or carefully **3. learn by heart** = memorize **4. she barked** = yelled **5. Neville was rising straight up like a cork out of a bottle** = rising up into the air quickly **6. He'd walked into a nightmare** = found himself in a terrible, scary situation **7. shoveling pie into his mouth** = eating a large amount of pie quickly **8. moonlight caught them** = moonlight shined on them, making them stand out in the dark

**Page 34:** Answers will vary.

| | Event | Feelings Associated with the Event | Adjectives or Phrases Used by the Author |
|---|---|---|---|
| **1.** | The day Harry receives his new broomstick. | happy, thrilled, excited, etc. | "hiding his glee" |
| **2.** | Harry, Ron, and Hermione's battle with the troll. | frightened, afraid, exhilarated | "shrinking against the wall" "petrified scream" |
| **3.** | The lecture they receive from Professor McGonagall. | remorseful, regretful, sorry | "hope of winning points faded" "Harry looked at the floor" |
| **4.** | The revelation that they are now friends forever. | awkwardness | "embarrassed pause" |

# Answer Key

**Page 35:** Answers will vary. Sample answers are listed below.

**Soccer Only**
1 ball, shin guards,
11 players, 2 goals,
goal = 1 point,
field on the ground,
time limit

**Both**
Balls, points for goals,
goals, goalkeeper,
fields, penalties,
referees

**Quidditch Only**
4 balls, brooms, field in air,
7 players, 6 goals, goal = 10 points,
Snitch = 150 points, no time limit

**Page 36:** Answers will vary.

| | Event | Characters | Possible Conclusion |
|---|---|---|---|
| 1. | Vault 713 is emptied of a "grubby little package wrapped up in brown paper." | *Hagrid, Harry, Griphook* | *Hagrid is bringing the package to Hogwarts.* |
| 2. | Students are forbidden to use the third floor of Hogwarts. | *Dumbledore* | **There is something dangerous there.** |
| 3. | A three-headed dog is seen guarding a trapdoor. | **Harry, Ron, Hermione, Neville** | **Something important is hidden under the trapdoor.** |
| 4. | There is a troll loose in the school. | **Harry, Ron, Hermione** | **Someone sent it on purpose.** |
| 5. | Snape has a bad wound on his leg. | **Harry, Professor Snape, Filch** | **The three-headed dog bit him.** |
| 6. | There is something wrong with Harry's new broomstick. | **Harry, Hermione, Professor Snape, Ron, Professor Quirrell** | **Someone is trying to harm Harry.** |
| 7. | Hagrid mentions the name Nicolas Flamel | **Harry, Hermione, Ron, Hagrid** | *Nicolas Flamel is involved with the secret.* |

**Page 37:** Answers will vary.

**Page 38:** Answers will vary.

**Page 39:** Answers will vary.

**Page 40:**

**fanatic**—one who is excessively devoted to a cause
**spluttered**—spoke hastily as when confused or upset, making oneself hard to understand
**sinister**—suggesting evil or malicious intentions
**mystified**—confused; puzzled
**immortal**—to live forever
**biased**—to have an unfair opinion
**shifty**—untrustworthy
**suspicious**—questionable
**trowels**—small hand shovels with pointed blades used for digging and gardening
**furling**—wrapping or rolling up
**spiral**—circling around a center point
**alibis**—stories to defend one's innocence
**meddle**—interfere
**rebellion**—defiance against an authority

**furor**—a state of excitement
**dappled**—spotted
**imprecise**—not exact
**sweltering**—unbearably hot
**omen**—a sign of good or bad things to come
**skulking**—hiding; lurking
**tottered**—swayed as if about to stumble or fall down
**threshold**—an entrance or doorway
**loathed**—disliked greatly
**spasm**—a sudden involuntary movement
**petrified**—terrified; scared
**vain**—without success
**agony**—extreme pain
**hygienic**—clean and healthy
**sidled**—stepped sideways
**abysmal**—hopeless; very bad, as in a performance

**Page 41:**

**Chapter Thirteen: Nicolas Flamel**
**1.** He finds Flamel on a wizard card about Dumbledore in a Chocolate Frog wrapper. Flamel is 665 years old, lives in Devon, was Dumbledore's partner in alchemy, and the is owner and creator of the Sorcerer's Stone.
**2.** The Sorcerer's Stone will transform any metal into pure gold, and produces the Elixir of Life which will make the drinker immortal.
**3.** "If brains were gold you'd be poorer than Weasley." It means that since Ron Weasley is very poor, Neville has no brains.
**4.** Neville stood up to Draco Malfoy, who continued to taunt Neville and Ron until Ron hit Draco Malfoy. Crabbe and Goyle and Neville joined in.
**5.** He flew over the forest to spy on Snape and Quirrell.
**6.** The Sorcerer's Stone was being guarded by the monstrous dog, Fluffy. Harry overhears Snape ask Quirrell if he has figured out how to get past Fluffy. Harry shares the news with Hermione and Ron.

**Chapter Fourteen: Norbert the Norwegian Ridgeback**
**7.** Harry, Ron, and Hermione give him encouraging smiles, and told people off if they made fun of him and his stutter.
**8.** Hagrid is reading books about the care of dragons. He is hatching a dragon egg in his cabin.
**9.** Hermione uses a flattering voice and mentioned that she wondered who Dumbledore trusts enough to guard the stone.
**10.** Hagrid and Dumbledore know how to get the Stone.
**11.** Ron writes ask Charlie to take the dragon to Romania. Charlie promises to send friends on Saturday night to pick up the dragon.
**12.** Norbert is the dragon. He is hoisted through the air by Charlie's friends on broomsticks.
**13.** They are relieved that they don't have to worry about Hagrid and the dragon, and Malfoy received a detention. Then, they get caught by Filch because they forget the invisibility cloak.

**Chapter Fifteen: The Forbidden Forest**
**14.** Gryffindor students ignore and taunt him. Hufflepuffs and Ravenclaws did as well, because they want Slytherin to lose the house cup. Slytherin students cheer for him.
**15.** Harry has to go into the forest for detention. He meets centaurs (Ronan, Baine, Firenze) and a horrible, hooded creature.

**Chapter Fifteen: The Forbidden Forest (continued)**
**16.** A hooded creature sipping unicorn blood sees Harry and walks toward him threateningly.
**17.** Firenze protects Harry and explains that unicorn blood keeps you alive but gives you a cursed half-life. Firenze says the planets warn of danger, but he hopes they are wrong.

**Chapter Sixteen: Through the Trapdoor**
**18.** Harry is still having nightmares about the green, flashing life, but now a blood-dripping, hooded figure also appears in them. He believes that Voldemort is coming back, and that is why his scar hurts.
**19.** Harry believes that Snape will try to steal the Sorcerer's Stone.
**20.** Ron and Hermione go with Harry to get the Sorcerer's Stone, even though it is dangerous.
**21.** Hagrid uses Fluffy, the three-headed dog; Professor Sprout uses the Devil's Snare (a plant that wraps around people); Professor Flitwick charms some winged keys, Professor McGonagall creates a life-sized chessboard with live pieces; Professor Quirrell uses a troll as a guardian; Professor Snape uses a logic puzzle with potions; and Professor Dumbledore uses the mirror of Erised.
**22.** Harry and his friends use the flute Hagrid gave him to sing Fluffy to sleep. They use fire to burn away the Devil's Snare. They catch the right key riding broomsticks. Ron, Harry, and Hermione become chess pieces, and Ron guides them through the chess game. The troll is unconscious already. Hermione solves the potions puzzle.

**Chapter Seventeen: The Forbidden Forest**
**23.** Harry finds Professor Quirrell in the last chamber. Quirrell tells Harry that he (Quirrell) set the troll loose in the castle on Halloween. He says that Snape was trying to scare him, but was not after the stone.
**24.** The Mirror of Erised is there to protect the Sorcerer's Stone. Harry only desires to have the stone, not to use it, so it appears in his pocket.
**25.** Gryffindor won the most house points because of Harry's bravery, Ron's chess game, Hermione's logic, and Neville's courage to stand up to his friends. The Gryffindor, Hufflepuff, and Ravenclaw students are no longer angry at him for losing house points.

**Page 42:** Flamel was born in 1331. Other answers will vary.

**Page 43:** Answers will vary.

**Page 44:** Answers will vary.

**Page 45:** Answers will vary.

**Page 46:**
**Continent:** Europe
**Location:** 46° North, 25° East
**Population:** 22,432,000
**Size:** 91,699 square miles
**Capital:** Bucharest
**Bordering Countries:**
Bulgaria, Yugoslavia,
Serbia, Ukraine. Moldova

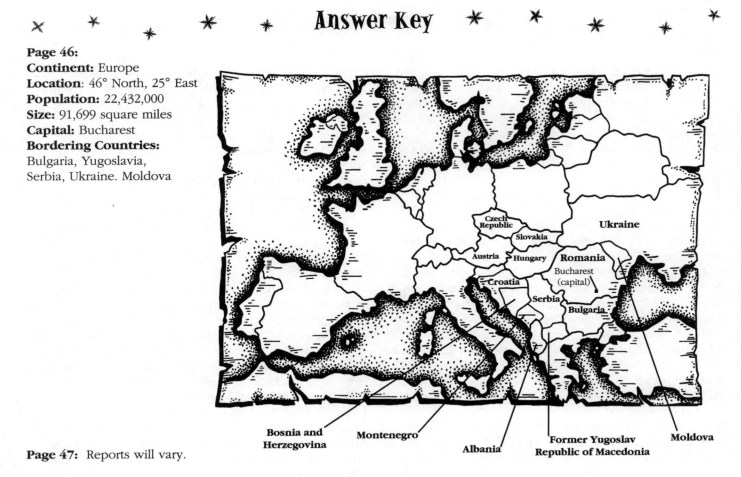

**Page 47:** Reports will vary.

**Page 48:** Answers will vary. See below for general information about unicorns and centaurs.
**Unicorns:** The word comes from Latin and means "one-horned." Traditionally, unicorns are the same size and shape as horses, are always white, and have a single horn protruding from their foreheads. In mythology, unicorns have magical powers, such as healing. There are references to unicorns in many cultures, including Ancient Rome, Asia, and the Bible.
**Centaurs:** In mythology, these creatures have the body of a horse and the head and torso of a man. Sometimes portrayed as evil, they are usually depicted as less-than-civilized, especially in their use of wine and treatment of women. The first mention of them is found around 2000 B.C., and may have originated from the first sightings of men on horseback.

**Page 49:** Answers will vary, but should relate to the subject taught by each professor. **Professor Sprout:** Herbology; **Professor Binns:** History of Magic; **Professor Flitwick**: Charms; **Professor Quirrell:** Defense Against the Dark Arts; **Professor McGonagall:** Transfiguration; **Professor Snape:** Potions; **Professor Dumbledore:** Hogwarts Headmaster

**Page 50:** There are many ways to explain the unusual properties of the cornstarch and water mixture. It is a natural polymer (a substance that forms when many of the same molecule attach together in rows). The mixture has a viscosity (fluidity) that is pressure-sensitive. The students should reach the conclusion that it appears to have magical abilities because the mixture is resistant to pressure, and yet, at the same time, flows like a liquid.

**Page 51:** **1.** The Dark Forces (55 Galleons) **2.** Fantastic Beasts and Where To Find Them (50 Galleons) **3.** Magical Drafts and Potions (36 Galleons) **4.** Beginners Guide To Transfiguration (35 Galleons) **5.** The Standard Book of Spells (25 Galleons) **6.** One Thousand Magical Herbs and Fungi (19 Galleons) **7.** Magical Theory (18 Galleons) **8.** A History of Magic (10 Galleons)

**Page 52:** Predictions will vary.